NEXT-LEVEL NEEDLEPOINT

NEXT-LEVEL NEEDLEPOINT

Over 100 skill-building stitches and techniques for modern tapestry embroidery

EMMA HOMENT

DAVID & CHARLES
— PUBLISHING —

www.davidandcharles.com

CONTENTS

INTRODUCTION

After all the love for my first book, *Needlepoint: A Modern Stitch Directory*, I thought it only right to bring you a collection of even more exciting stitches and techniques to try. So, get ready to take your needlepoint to the next level as we explore the world of dynamic and textural stitches. *Next-Level Needlepoint* will give you the confidence to start making bold stitching choices that will bring your needlepoint to life.

I've curated my selection of over 100 stitches into brilliantly self-explanatory sections, focused on providing answers to your stitching prayers. Looking for something to bring flow to your design? **Movement** is full of energetic stitches that flaunt their direction to do just that. Needing an option to break up a block of stitching? **Texture** has so many tactile choices for eye-catching dimension.

Wishing you could capture realistic details in your stitched pictures? Let me introduce you to the world of 'scenic stitches', decorative stitches that really tell the story of the space they're filling. Snowy stitches, cloud shapes, even lightning bolts are just a few of the aerial wonders to be found in **Sky**. Subtle ripples on a pond or bold waves on the sea, even underwater bubbles, these and more aquatic delights can be achieved with the pick of **Water**. Tree canopies, wheat fields, sand dunes, flower borders, all can be replicated in stitch with the possibilities in **Land**. I'm asked for help in these areas more than any other, so I hope you'll love the ones I've selected – they're my absolute favourites!

Even the dedicated basketweave-stitchers among you are bound to be tempted by the gorgeous stitches in **Borders** that offer beautiful ways to frame your designs. There are so many choices here for you to get inspired by, and whatever you need, I've got you covered.

Whether you're a beginner or a seasoned stitcher, with my step-by-step guides, packed full of how-to illustrations and photographs of stitched samples, you'll want to turn your hand to trying out each and every one of them. And I've created 10 new projects too, bringing my love of bright, colourful, joy-filled designs to help you to explore and celebrate decorative stitches. I've chosen to stitch all the new designs in this book onto plastic canvas as it's such a versatile material and the finished projects can be made up quickly and easily. If, however, you prefer to stitch onto regular canvas, everything you'll need to know is included in **Getting Started**, such as advice on choosing and using a frame, and blocking stitched fabric.

I love to share new and exciting stitches with crafters, as I do in #stitchmondays, my Instagram showcase of needlepoint stitches. My hope is that you will take the stitches in this book far beyond these pages and start experimenting with them yourself, swapping them out for those in the kits you buy or the projects you make, to add your own creative twist to any needlepoint design you stitch.

www.instagram.com/themakersmarks

WHAT IS NEEDLEPOINT?

Whether you are crazy for cross stitch or nutty for needlepoint, you are an embroidery enthusiast, because essentially everything is embroidery. Confused? Well, let me explain...

Imagine an umbrella. At the cap at the top sits 'embroidery', a word that captures all stitches worked on any type of surface. Arcing down from the cap, on one side of the canopy is what we traditionally recognize as embroidery, the delicate little stitches worked on a tightly woven evenweave fabric, such as calico, cotton or linen. Arcing down on the other side of the canopy is needlepoint, often using similar stitches to those you find in embroidery, but this time worked on lovely open weave canvas. Forking off from the needlepoint curve (imagine them as the panels of your umbrella), you'll find cross stitch and Bargello, needlepoint stitches striking out to do their own thing.

So, the material you decide to stitch on pretty much tells you which craft you're doing. Though let's be honest, crafting rules are there to be broken. If you can find anything with an even set of holes across it, you'll find a crafter prepared to stitch it. Chain-link fences make for excellent stitch installations!

While the fabric you work your stitches on flags up the type of needlework you are doing, do the fibres you use threaded through your needle dictate the craft in the same way? Well, that used to be the case. Traditionally, needlepoint, or 'tapestry needlepoint' as it was more commonly known across Europe, was stitched using wool. And while most needlepoint kits still come packaged with wool to stitch your design in, these days any fibre can find its place on a needlepoint canvas - even ribbon!

Needlepoint isn't a modern craft, by any means. While we can trace its roots back as far as the Ancient Egyptians, needlepoint really became a main player on the craft stage in the 16th century and has continued to have groundbreaking moments in every century since. The 17th century saw the rise of Bargello, named after the palace in Florence in which it was found adorning chairs. With the growing interest in and popularization of upholstered furniture, there was a big opportunity to add embellishment, and it's in moments like these that different forms of embroidery find space to grow.

In the 18th century, needlepoint became a teaching tool, a way to hone so-called 'ladylike' skills in young women and girls, and this was the golden age of the traditional 'sampler'. The sampler was a way stitchers could show off different stitch techniques in a single piece of work, often incorporating alphabets and numerals as well as motifs personal to the stitcher. The earliest samplers that have been discovered are Peruvian, dating back as far as 200BCE–300CE, and while they must have been stitched across the world from this point onwards, the majority that have survived are European and North American.

In the 19th century came the Industrial Revolution and with it the craft world saw the arrival of Berlin woolwork, a new style of needlework stitched in tent stitch to create bold, bright, colourful designs in multiple tones and shades, all made possible by new fibre-dyeing techniques often using chemical-based colourants. This is also when we start to see charted designs being created and shared, similar to the ones we use today, and this made needlepoint accessible and affordable for the masses. Berlin woolwork designers took inspiration from the paintings of the time, with many designs featuring florals, animals and birds, although geometric patterns did manage to creep in, too.

Despite these landmark moments in the history of needlepoint, there must be so much we don't know. Any craft made using natural materials runs the risk of perishing over time. Without records for us to refer to, it's as though something never existed, so it's quite possible that needlepoint had a part to play in other cultures, but that this has now been lost in the mists of time - well, at least for now!

GETTING STARTED

TOOLS AND MATERIALS

For needlepoint, all you really need is an open weave canvas, a tapestry needle and a thread to stitch with. But for those three things there are a variety of choices to make, so here is a quick introduction to what you need to know.

CANVAS

You'll need something to stitch onto, of course, and in the needlepoint world you'll come across a few different types of canvas more regularly than others. When you see a listing for canvas you'll normally see a number followed by either 'hpi' or 'ct', which stand for 'holes per inch' and 'count', but these mean exactly the same thing; so if you have a 12-ct or 12-hpi canvas, it means that there are 12 holes in your canvas for every inch. A piece of 12-ct canvas, for example, will have more, and therefore smaller, holes than a piece of 8-ct canvas.

Mono interlock canvas

This is my favourite type of canvas. Made from natural fibres, it is a single thread (hence 'mono') woven canvas in which the vertical threads are bound around each horizontal thread to lock them in place (hence 'interlock'). The interlocked canvas strands mean that the weave is stabilized so there is minimal fraying at its edges. The weave process means the surface of the canvas lies flat, making it perfect for digital printing, and this is the canvas most commonly used in UK-produced needlepoint kits.

Select your canvas based on its mesh size (the number of holes per inch): 12-ct is the perfect choice for designs worked in tent stitch with tapestry wool or in cross stitch with crewel wool. For designs worked in cross stitch with tapestry wool, use 10-ct canvas; if you use 12-ct, the stitches will appear too tightly compacted and they will become difficult to stitch as tapestry wool fibre is too thick for the job. It's important to find a compatible fit between the thread you choose to stitch with and the canvas count you're stitching onto. As a general rule, the more times a stitch or set of stitches has to pass through the same canvas hole, the thinner the thread needs to be.

Mono canvas

This type of canvas has a weft strand going over and under a warp thread, giving the canvas a bumpy surface texture, and it's often seen in the hand-painted designer canvases produced in the US. It lacks the structure that interlocking gives, so you will need to use a low-tack artist's tape to bind the edges to avoid fraying.

YOU WILL NOTICE THE MORE YOU WORK WITH YOUR WOVEN CANVASES THE SOFTER THEY WILL BECOME. THIS IS PERFECTLY NORMAL.

Plastic canvas

This is a poured and stamped piece of soft flexible plastic that's really easy to stitch onto. Because it's not woven like mono and mono interlock canvas, it holds its shape perfectly, making it a great choice when you're just starting to learn needlepoint. However, one thing to be aware of is that plastic canvas has thicker bars and intersections than woven canvas, and this means that a 12-ct plastic canvas can be a tight squeeze for tapestry wool, which always glides perfectly through a 12-ct natural canvas, so you may need to switch to 10-ct.

A 10-CT PLASTIC CANVAS IS PERFECT FOR BARGELLO PROJECTS AS IT GIVES GREAT COVERAGE FOR STRAIGHT STITCHES.

PLASTIC CANVAS

MONO CANVAS

MONO INTERLOCK CANVAS

21-CT CANVAS STITCHED WITH 2-PLY WEIGHT CREWEL WOOL

10-CT PLASTIC CANVAS STITCHED WITH 4-PLY WEIGHT TAPESTRY WOOL

12-CT CANVAS STITCHED WITH RICO RUMI CROCHET COTTON

THREADS

The thickness of the thread you choose to stitch with is very much dictated by the canvas count and the coverage you're looking to achieve. Standard tapestry wools from Anchor, DMC and Appletons (the brands most often found in kits) are perfect for 12-ct canvas, but there are so many more fibre choices out there to discover. Some of my favourites are Planet Earth Fiber, Rainbow Gallery and Kreinik. However, you might need to double up the thickness to achieve the right coverage.

What do we mean by 'coverage'? Well, it's when we're talking about how much canvas is peeking through the stitches. Most kits and designs are worked to full coverage, where stitches completely cover the canvas, but sometimes you'll use a decorative stitch that allows for intermittent coverage, enabling you to play with texture.

Whichever thread choice you make, there are a couple of things that you should look out for. Consider thread length: Anchor and Appletons skeins come in 10m (11yd) lengths, for example, whereas DMC skeins are 8m (8¾yd) long, something to be aware of if you are going to embark on larger projects – there's nothing worse than running out of wool when you only have a small section of canvas left! Be aware of the dye lot number, too: if you are working on a project that requires more than one skein of the same colour, it's really important to make sure you have the same dye lot number as you'll spot the difference when you start stitching!

It is also worth noting that tapestry wool is spun with a particularly dense twist, which makes it a lot less stretchy than knitting yarn. While you can substitute tapestry wool with DK knitting yarn, you must be very mindful of your stitch tension because of the stretch. Vegan stitchers might be interested to know that I have found Rico Rumi crochet cotton to be the best vegan substitute for tapestry wool in terms of like-for-like coverage.

NEVER USE A MIX OF THREAD BRANDS FOR THE SAME COLOURED AREA OF CANVAS: EACH HAS A DIFFERENT DYEING PROFILE SO, WHEN PLACED ALONGSIDE EACH OTHER, YOU'LL SEE SUBTLETIES IN TONE.

12-CT CANVAS STITCHED WITH 2-PLY WEIGHT CREWEL WOOL

12-CT CANVAS STITCHED WITH 4-PLY WEIGHT TAPESTRY WOOL

10-CT PLASTIC CANVAS STITCHED WITH 2-PLY WEIGHT CREWEL WOOL

7-CT CANVAS STITCHED WITH DOUBLED-UP 4-PLY WEIGHT TAPESTRY WOOL

NEEDLES

Tapestry needles have a large eye for threading your fibres through and a blunt end that makes it easier to stitch with. The needle passes smoothly through the canvas and is much less likely to catch and snag on your fibres or pierce your canvas bars.

The size of needle required depends on the hole count of the canvas you are using (see table for a general guide, although you may choose to go up or down a size depending on what is more comfortable for you); the higher the number the finer the needle. Go for a tried and tested needle maker. With cheaper, less well-known brands, you run the danger that the needles may snap or tarnish easily. The most popular brands are Bohin, Tulip and, my personal favourite, John James.

Holes Per Inch (hpi)	Needle Size
8hpi to 10hpi	Size 16
10hpi to 12hpi	Size 18
12hpi to 14hpi	Size 20
14hpi to 18hpi	Size 22
22hpi to 24hpi	Size 24 to 26

NOTIONS

One of the best things about being a crafter is the stash! I'm a sucker for a cute needlepoint accessory, but let's remind ourselves of a few stitching essentials.

Embroidery scissors

Whether you choose a brightly coloured, fun-shaped pair or a classic stork set, you'll definitely need embroidery scissors in your needlepoint life. These are much smaller than your average scissors, for ease of manoeuvrability. Their sharp, precise blades cut threads neatly, making needle threading easier. I know a lot of stitchers who are partial to a pair of 'snips', which look like mini sheep shears, and these are an increasingly popular choice.

Needle minders and pin cushions

My friend Genevieve first introduced me to needle minders and I am now obsessed! A needle minder is a type of metal badge with a magnet underneath instead of a pin. You take the top badge section and rest it on the top of the canvas, then pop the magnet underneath, essentially sandwiching the canvas in between, giving you a place to keep your needle safe between stitching sessions. So, no more weaving needles into the canvas for safe keeping, or losing them down the sofa! They come in so many wonderful designs that are very collectible. Of course, a pin cushion does the job too and is the perfect excuse to add a statement piece to your craft stash!

Frames

Whether you choose to stitch with your fabric in a frame or not is entirely up to you. It really comes down to your own comfort. Some stitchers prefer to stitch without a frame, keeping the project held in the hand. And if you're stitching on plastic canvas, a frame is not required at all. If you do choose the handheld route, then you may notice a little warp in the canvas when you've finished. But don't worry, as this slight wonkiness can be fixed easily by a process called blocking (see How to Stitch).

I prefer to use a frame as it gives the canvas a lovely even tension that I find makes it easier to stitch: a taut canvas will allow your needle to slip through the canvas holes really smoothly.

There are several different types of frame to choose from including scroll frames, bar frames and clip frames. Your choice will depend on what feels right with the way you stitch and where you sit to do your needlepoint. Let's consider the options.

Scroll frames These are the most expensive option and the bulkiest. There are several different types including lap stands, floor stands and table stands. They consist of two side panels and a pair of rollers, available in a range of widths. The rollers have a strip of canvas for stitching the fabric onto and work is usually left on the frame until finished (see Preparing to Stitch for more details). They can be heavy, so not the best choice for smaller projects.

Bar frames These are a more cost-effective option, and the size can be adjusted according to your project size using interchangeable side lengths. They can be handheld or attached to a stand, but the bigger the bar frame, the more likely it is that you'll need to attach it to a stand.

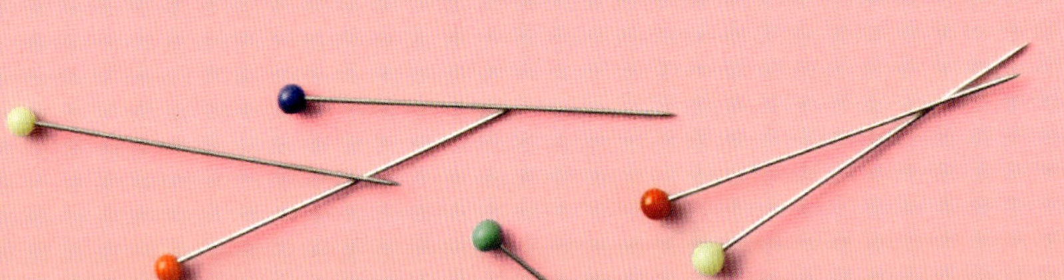
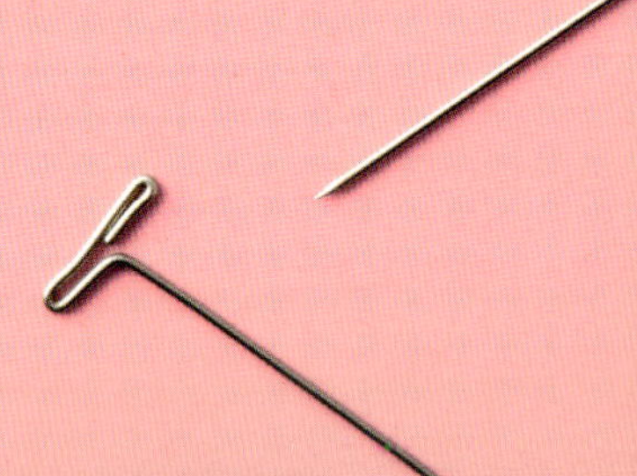

Clip frames These are relatively inexpensive and definitely the easiest to travel with. It's so simple to unclip the sides and roll up your work to pop it in a project bag. They are my go-to frame as they are so lightweight and their modular tube lengths are so adaptable.

Stands Many scroll frames come with a stand, but even bar and clip frames can be easily attached to a stand if you don't enjoy stitching with the frame held in your hand. Lowery have stands that make hands-free stitching a pleasure, available in lovely bright colours. They have a clamping arm that you fix to your frame to raise it up to a comfortable height, allowing you to stitch with two hands.

Before making a frame purchase, see if a friend has one you can try or ask for a demonstration at your local sewing store. For step-by-step advice on framing up your fabric, see Preparing to Stitch.

AN EMBROIDERY HOOP IS NOT SUITABLE FOR NEEDLEPOINT EMBROIDERY! IT WILL BUCKLE YOUR CANVAS FABRIC WITHOUT GIVING THE EVEN TENSION YOU NEED.

PREPARING TO STITCH

I'm a fan of stitching with my fabric in a frame so I've provided a guide here to framing up your fabric into three different types of frame. Also, before you can begin stitching, you'll need to organize your threads.

PREPARING A SCROLL FRAME

01 Stitch the top edge of your canvas to the strip of webbing running along the top bar.

02 Stitch the bottom edge of your canvas to the strip of webbing running along the bottom bar.

03 Turn the bars until the canvas is rolled around them to show the piece of the design that you're ready to stitch first. If you are stitching a larger design you may find you need to keep some of it rolled up, only rolling out a section at a time. As you roll to show the area to be worked on next, you will roll up the canvas area that has already been stitched on.

PREPARING A BAR FRAME

If you are using mono canvas, first edge your canvas with artist's tape to prevent it from fraying. Artist's tape is a low tack tape so it won't leave any sticky residue. Mono interlocking canvas is very unlikely to fray, so it does not require taping.

01 Construct the bar frame by carefully slotting the corner joints together. (Different lengths of bars can be slotted together to match your fabric size.)

02 Pin your prepared fabric onto the bars using thumb tacks, pulling the fabric taut, working from the centre of each bar to the edge.

03 I prefer to stitch with the bars underneath my design, so I can curl my fingers underneath as I hold the frame. But I know other stitchers like the bars on top. Just choose what feels most comfortable to you.

PREPARING A CLIP FRAME

01 Clip frames are best used to match the size of your project. Slot your tubes together.

02 Making sure your canvas is at least 2.5cm (1in) larger on all sides than your frame, place your canvas on top of the frame, then use the clips to 'clip' it in to place.

03 As your canvas softens it may lose some tension in the frame; to re-tighten just twist the clips towards the back of your frame.

ORGANIZING YOUR THREADS

Needlepoint threads come in skeins, hanks, spools and cards. Each has its own knack for unravelling the ends so you can cut a length.

For cards and spools The thread will be tucked into a little cut-out groove. Take the end of your needle and gently tease it loose.

For skeins and hanks Take off the paper band and find the end of the thread. Don't be tempted to pull the end with the paper band still on, as you'll get caught up in a big tangly mess.

If you are working on a large project, it can be a good idea to cut all your thread lengths in one go, so a thread organizer or large bobbins are a good idea for keeping them until you need them.

Thread organizer A panel with a series of holes in it, ready for you to loop your threads over in colour blocks, although you can easily make your own by punching holes into a strong piece of cardboard.

Large bobbins As tapestry wools are thicker, a standard embroidery cardboard bobbin won't hold a great deal, but most large acrylic bobbins can hold a full 10m (11yd) skein. Stick on little labels to record your colour reference and dye lot number.

TO CUT A PERFECT LENGTH OF THREAD TO COMFORTABLY STITCH WITH, SIMPLY HOLD THE END OF THE WOOL IN YOUR FINGERTIP, STRETCH IT TO THE CROOK OF YOUR ARM, THEN SNIP.

HOW TO STITCH

Here you'll find all you need to get stitching, from how to read a chart to starting and finishing your threads. There are handy hints on how to keep your stitches looking neat, your project backs tidy, and what to do if you do happen to pop any stitches in the wrong place. Don't worry, soon this will all be second nature to you.

HOW TO READ A CHART

The majority of the charted designs featured in this book are shown as stitched, which makes them easy to follow. On a couple of occasions though, on the Rise and Shine Mirror for example, you may see the background of the chart left as blank squares for the sake of clarity.

Each square represents a canvas intersection, where the warp and the weft of the canvas cross over each other. So if you're working a project in one of the tent stitches, or any stitch worked across perfect diagonals, it's really easy to work out how many stitches you will be making, as shown in the chart and stitched sample 1.

If you're working with straight stitches, like double woven stitch for example, rather than working across intersections of canvas, you'll be going over the canvas bars (the threads of canvas in between the intersections). In this case, each square will represent your thread crossing over a canvas bar, as shown in the chart and stitched sample 2.

When you are using decorative stitches that stretch themselves over bars and intersections at varying lengths, then your squares become an indicator of the area of canvas to cover. This is where your judgement comes in to play and you may find that you need to add some compensating stitches to perfectly fill the area. The chart and stitched sample 3 show two types of stitch sitting together.

Compensating stitches are when you use part of a decorative stitch to finish off the row or column of stitches when there isn't enough space left on the canvas to do the full stitch, as shown in the chart and stitched sample 4. These can be a really useful way of helping to get a tricky shape just right. More on that later.

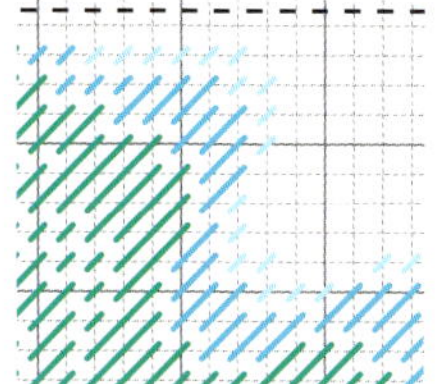

1. DIAGONAL STITCHES: CHART AND STITCH SAMPLE FROM BESIDE THE SEA BEACH BAG.

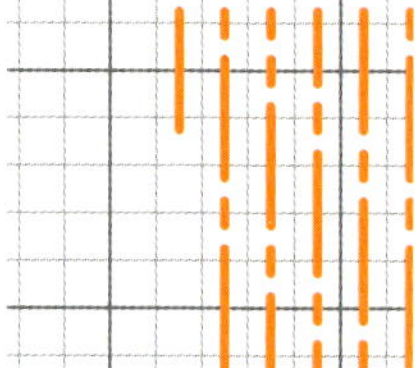

2. HORIZONTAL AND VERTICAL STITCHES: CHART AND STITCH SAMPLE FROM RISE AND SHINE MIRROR FRAME.

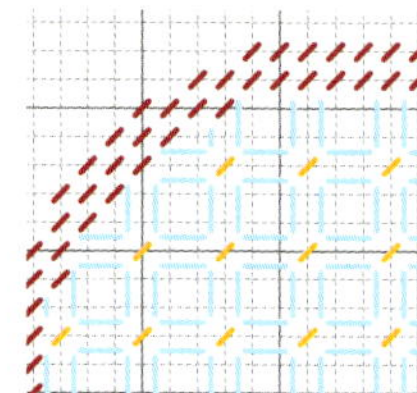

3. COMBINATION STITCHES: CHART AND STITCH SAMPLE FROM FOR THE LOVE OF FLOWERS NOTEBOOK.

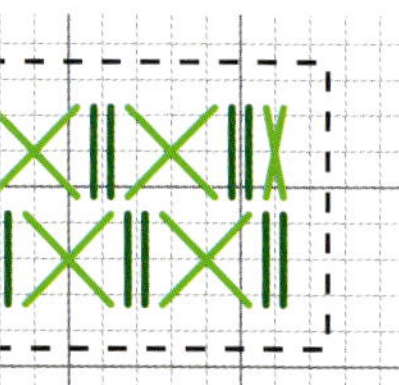

4. COMPENSATING STITCHES: CHART AND STITCH SAMPLE FROM LITTLE TREASURES TRINKET TRAY.

CASTING ON

Casting on is the expression I use for starting a new thread ready to begin your needlepoint. There are lots of ways to get started, but I like the waste knot method best.

Thread your needle and tie a knot at the end of the length of thread. Bring the needle through the front of your canvas about six canvas holes from the direction you will be stitching in. You will be able to see your knot on the front of the canvas. Start to sew towards the waste knot, making sure to go over the thread length that leads from the waste knot (which can be seen at the back of the canvas), essentially trapping the thread in. Then, when you're a stitch away from the waste knot, just snip it off. Your thread end is safe and secure!

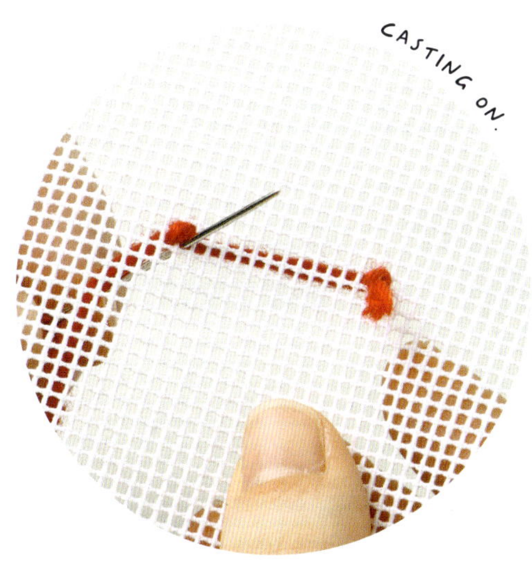

CASTING ON.

CASTING OFF

Casting off is the expression I use for finishing the thread, either because you have completed the area of stitching or because you need to start a new length of thread. By far the easiest way to cast off is to run your needle through the back of your stitches, pulling the end of your thread along with it for about 2cm (¾in). This will tuck your thread into the back of the stitching and you can then safely snip off any excess.

WHENEVER POSSIBLE, CAST OFF STITCHES THROUGH THE BACKS OF STITCHES OF THE SAME COLOUR, TO PREVENT SHOW-THROUGH ON THE FRONT OF THE PIECE.

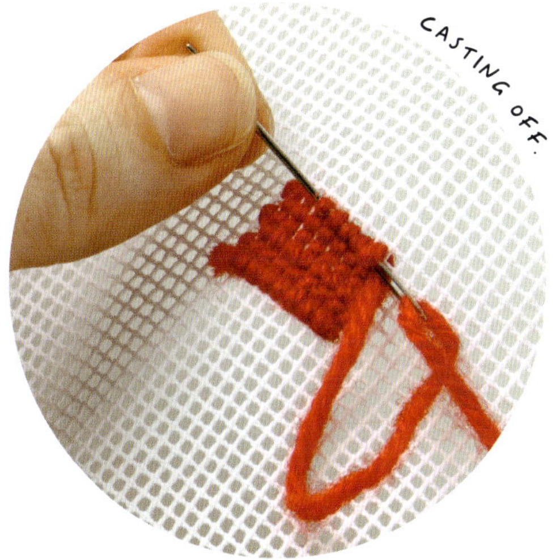

CASTING OFF.

PARKING THREADS

Mastering the art of 'parking' your threads is a great trick to have up your stitching sleeve, especially when you're working on projects that require a lot of colour changes in quick succession.

Let's take the Cute Card Keeper Wallet as an example: at the start of the stitching, there are a lot of quick colour changes for the stripes; you'll start stitching in yellow but soon move on to peach, then orange and back to peach before returning to yellow to continue the alternating stripe pattern. Casting off the yellow thread when you'll soon be using it again would waste thread, not to mention the frustration of having to stop and start each time. I'd take my yellow thread length and 'park' it higher up and out of the way of the direction I will be stitching next (see photo). Then I'd cast on my peach thread, stitch this area, then park that thread, to move on to the orange thread. For the next stripe, I'll 'unpark' my peach thread and continue as before. Easy peasy!

PARKING THREADS.

THE BACK OF YOUR WORK

Unless you've done a course at the Royal School of Needlework, it's unlikely that the back of your work will look as neat as the front. Some people achieve super-neat backs, while for others the reverse of their pieces look like a pile of spaghetti - but whichever you are, don't worry. There are just two key things to remember: never leave knots at the back of your work, as these create a lumpy surface that pushes up the front of your design; and never travel threads, especially dark ones, across the back of your canvas for a long distance as, if you do, you run the risk of accidentally pulling little bits of the thread through to the front side.

EXAMPLE OF PROJECT BACK.

BE CAREFUL WHEN TRAVELLING THREADS ACROSS THE BACK OF YOUR WORK – DON'T GO TOO FAR OR THE BACK OF YOUR WORK MAY GET IN A BIT OF A TANGLE.

STITCH TENSION

When making your stitches, you don't need to pull your tapestry wool tightly, but just enough to make sure the stitch isn't baggy. Each stitch should fit snugly against the canvas. You'll soon get into a rhythm with it and it will become very relaxing.

UNPICKING SMALL AREAS.

UNPICKING

There will be occasions when you have to unpick your stitches. No one's perfect, after all, and there will be times when you stitch a colour in the wrong place or miscount a pattern; but don't panic - we can fix it!

If you've just gone a few stitches wrong, slide your needle off your thread and carefully scoop your needle underneath the last stitch you worked from the top of the canvas. Gently pull your thread out from the canvas hole and continue until all the wrong stitches have been removed. Then simply rethread your needle and carefully go through the top of your canvas at the hole the thread is coming out from to bring your thread out at the back of your canvas, and you are ready to start stitching again.

If you have a large area of incorrect stitches, the method that works best is 'frogging', where a seam un-picker is used to rip through the stitches on the front of the canvas. This can be tricky and you must be very careful not to catch any of the canvas fibres or they will rip.

UNPICKING LARGE AREAS.

INVEST IN A PROJECT BAG TO KEEP YOUR CANVAS AND THREADS NEAT AND FLUFF FREE BETWEEN STITCH SESSIONS. SCOOP UP ALL YOUR NOTIONS INTO IT, TOO, SO THAT YOU HAVE EVERYTHING TO HAND.

BLOCKING

When your stitching is finished, you might find your canvas is a little warped and distorted, particularly if you haven't used a frame. One of the benefits of using plastic canvas, as I have for all the projects in this book, is that it holds its structure perfectly so this is not an issue. However, should you to choose to stitch on regular canvas, this handy guide will teach you everything you need to know to fix this using a process known as 'blocking'. Blocking can be done either wet or dry, but I prefer dry blocking as wet blocking can be a little risky unless your threads are completely dye fast.

First, get yourself some blocking mats (KnitIQ have amazing ones). These are square, soft mats that have grid lines printed on them. They have edges like jigsaw pieces so that they are easy to slot together for blocking bigger projects. They are usually supplied with a box of T pins. (Alternatively, you can draw some grid lines on a cork board for a DIY version.)

01 Remove any artist's tape (if used) from the edges of your canvas, then carefully line up the top corners of your needlepoint embroidery with the grid lines on the blocking mat and pin them in place, with your pin leaning out at an angle and your canvas pulled taut.

02 You may find it easier to start from one corner and pin along one edge first, gently teasing your canvas in line. Pins should be about 3cm (1⅛in) apart for the best effect. Make sure your pins are placed close to the stitched design and not to the edge of the canvas itself.

03 It can take as little as a couple of days or as much as a week to successfully block a project, so check in on the blocking progress of your canvas every couple of days. As the canvas starts to stretch back into place you may find you have to re-pin and adjust.

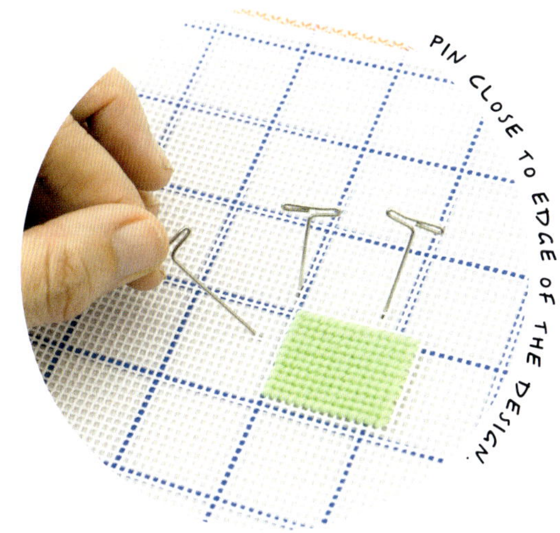

PIN CLOSE TO EDGE OF THE DESIGN.

GETTING CREATIVE

Now that we have covered all the things you need to start needlepointing as well as the practicalities of how to stitch, it's time to get creative!

There are more than 100 stitches for you to experiment with, as well as 10 projects that show you how you can begin to use some of these creative stitches. Each project comes with a chart and step-by-step guide, which you'll find easy to follow. But do you know what the exciting thing with a chart is? You have the option to go rogue!

When you see an area of any single colour on a chart, you could choose to change it to a different colour! Or you may think you'd actually rather use a different stitch from the one I used when I designed the project. Heck, you may just decide to stitch the whole thing in a simple tent stitch – it's totally up to you! For more advice on getting creative, see Choosing Your Stitches.

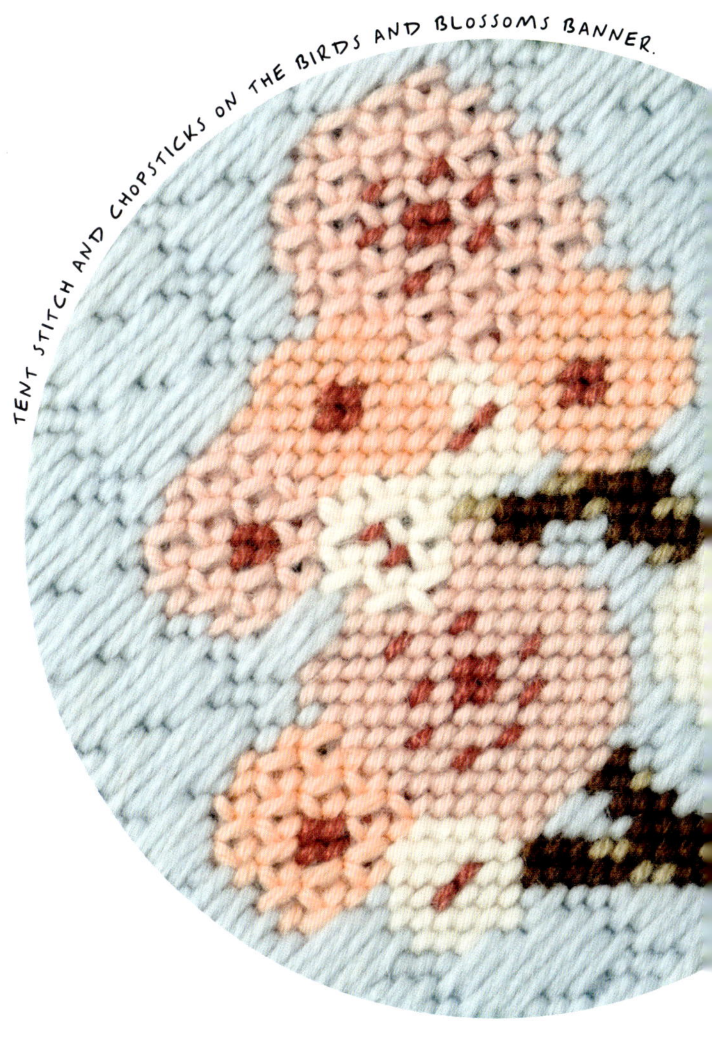

TENT STITCH AND CHOPSTICKS ON THE BIRDS AND BLOSSOMS BANNER.

CHOOSING YOUR STITCHES

With over 100 new stitches to choose from, you may be suffering from choice overload. How best to use them you may be asking yourself, and how do you identify those suitable for filling stitches that grab the attention, and those that might be better for bringing interest to backgrounds?

TENT STITCH BACKGROUND ON THE RISE AND SHINE MIRROR.

BACKGROUND STITCHES

Choosing a stitch to work in your backgrounds can be tricky. Do you go with something simple, as I did for the variegated-blue tent-stitch sky on the Rise and Shine Mirror Frame, or do you choose a bold themed choice, like the swirl stitch background on my Birds and Blossoms Banner, which calls to mind the puffiness of clouds?

The most important thing to remember with background stitches is not to let them pull the focus from your main design area. But that doesn't mean you have to always go small. A bold stitch can often make a perfect background choice (as does the soaring swirl stitch on my banner), just as long as the area of canvas to be worked is big enough to allow some breathing space. Backgrounds can be kept for small stitches, of course, and some stitchers may even prefer that; but they can often be a good area to be brave, allowing you the space to explore something a bit more substantial too.

SWIRL STITCH BACKGROUND ON THE BIRDS AND BLOSSOMS BANNER.

Sometimes you'll have a design that just feels like it needs to be stitched in a simple basketweave: maybe there are too many fiddly little areas to stitch, or perhaps you're just looking for a really mindful and relaxing repetitive stitch session. And there's absolutely nothing wrong with that. But before making a decision, take a look at my Beside the Sea Beach Bag design. Here I've used simple tent stitches for the details in my design - the message in a bottle, the shell and the starfishes - and I've chosen the bold sandhills stitch for the beach background. Rather than taking the focus away from my beach finds, this draws them to our attention by throwing them into relief.

As you grow familiar with the characteristics of each stitch, you'll find it easier to make choices with more confidence, and you'll soon develop a go-to list of your favourite backgrounds.

SANDHILLS STITCH BACKGROUND ON THE BESIDE THE SEA BEACH BAG.

STITCHES THAT LEAVE SOME EXPOSED CANVAS, SUCH AS DARNING STITCH FOR EXAMPLE, STITCH UP QUICKLY AND WORK BRILLIANTLY IN BACKGROUNDS, ESPECIALLY IF THE MAIN DESIGN IS MADE UP OF A SOLID BLOCK OF STITCHES.

FILLING STITCHES

Filling stitches are fabulous little stitches that you can use to fill an area on your canvas. It's true to say that, technically, all stitches are filling stitches, but here I'm particularly talking about those that help you fill a specifically shaped area, like the sun or the clouds on the Rise and Shine Mirror Frame for example. Let's take a look at filling stitches in a little more detail.

Some of the easiest filling stitches can be found in the tent stitch family, such as basketweave and continental stitch. Generally speaking, you'll find any stitch with small component parts, stretching over one or two canvas bars or intersections, is an easy one to fill with, and examples would include chopsticks and knit one, purl one.

Any stitch that travels on a perfect diagonal or horizontal line, staggered diagonals and diagonal pairs for example, will be super easy to negotiate into tricky shapes. The chances are you'll just have to shorten them when you reach the edges of your design area. This is classed as 'compensating' a stitch.

But just because there are easy choices doesn't mean you should limit yourself. I could have played it safe and used only tent stitch for the birds on the Birds and Blossoms Banner, but I wanted to choose stitches that would really bring them to life.

DETAIL OF RISING SUN FROM RISE AND SHINE MIRROR FRAME.

DETAIL OF FEATHERS FROM BIRDS AND BLOSSOMS BANNER.

Fill the shape, fire the imagination

When making your choice of stitch, you should be looking for two things: that it will fill up to the edges (or as near as) of the shape you have in mind, and that it will give you a texture that works with the overall design.

Personally, I love to use filling stitches that emulate the real-life qualities of the shapes I am stitching. So, for one of my four Elemental Coasters, I chose the aptly named grass stitch for the coaster representing earth.

But, if realism isn't your thing, you can have a lot of fun picking contrasting textural stitches, too. In fact there's a whole section of stitches in this book dedicated to adding amazing texture to your projects!

DETAIL OF GRASS STITCH ON ONE OF THE ELEMENTAL COASTERS.

HOLDING STITCHES IN ACTION.

To frame or not to frame? That is the question!

Filling stitches can hold a shape just as easily when left unframed as when framed with a 'holding' stitch like tent stitch. However, holding stitches certainly make it easier to define a shaped area and as such they can be to newbie stitchers what training wheels are to cycling novices.

You can incorporate holding stitches into your design by, for example, outlining an area in tent stitch using a contrast colour, then filling it with your chosen textural stitch. Alternatively, you can use *temporary* holding stitches to define an area as you work, to give you a line to work to as you adjust your chosen filling stitch to fit to its edges (see Compensating Stitches). Once this has been achieved, the temporary holding stitches are carefully removed. This is how I stitched the wings of the birds on the Birds and Blossoms Banner.

COMPENSATING STITCHES

Whatever your choice of background and filling stitches, you may find yourself in need of some compensating stitches. But what do I mean by compensating stitches?

Compensating stitches enable you to neatly finish right up to the edge of a shaped section. Sometimes, however, there isn't room to use the whole of the stitch, so you have to adapt the working of the stitch to use a partial section of it to finish off. So, for example, if you're stitching a row of upright cross stitches and find yourself running out of room at either end of the row, then the vertical part of the stitch forms a perfect compensating stitch – but if you're stitching a column, then the horizontal part of the stitch works best. In my Rise and Shine Mirror design the left-hand cloud is worked in double Hungarian stitch, normally worked across lengths of two and four bars of canvas. But you'll see that as I approach the top of the cloud design I'm having to shorten these lengths down to work across one, two or three bars of canvas.

Compensating stitches can often feel a little bit scary, so when in doubt, find yourself some gridded paper and a pencil, draw your defined edge and then sketch out how your stitch will travel towards it. This can really help you to visualize what you're up against as you take to the canvas. It's another great way to empower yourself as a stitcher. Trust me, there's nothing you can't tackle!

COMPENSATING STITCHES ON CLOUD FROM RISE AND SHINE MIRROR FRAME.

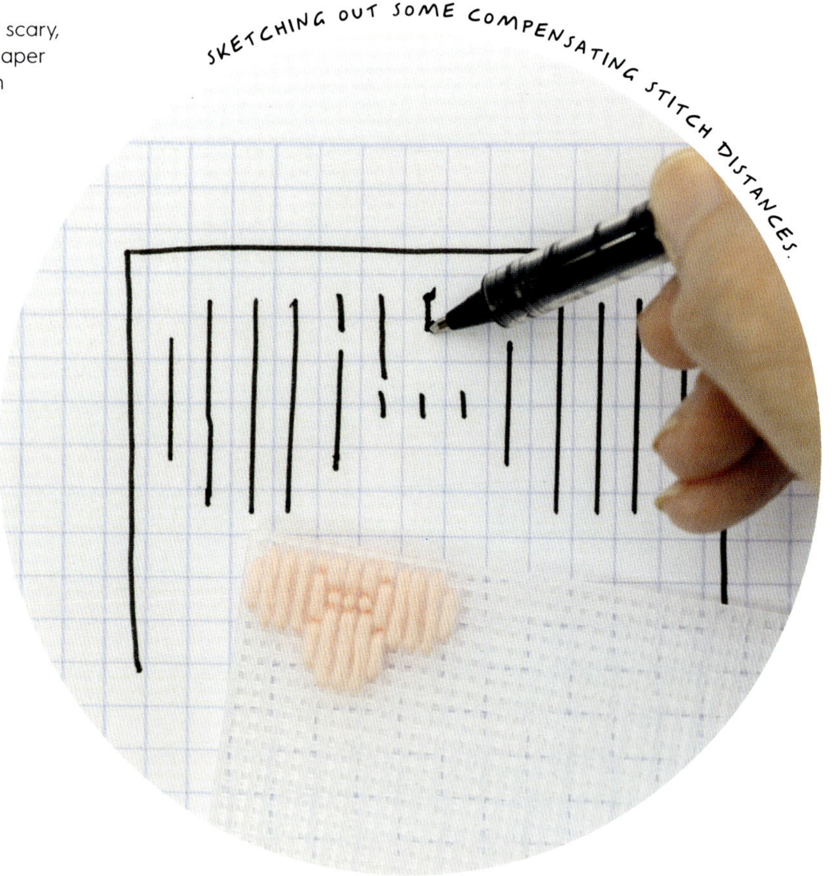

SKETCHING OUT SOME COMPENSATING STITCH DISTANCES.

CONTEXT IS EVERYTHING!

When choosing background and filling stitches, think about the context of the area you are stitching. What story do you want to tell in your choice of stitches? Are you looking to create a sense of movement, or to explore a specific texture? Movement stitches are all about the way they travel across the canvas, whether that is achieved in the direction they are actually stitched in, or the illusion they give as you build them up in a block. Textured stitches, on the other hand, are all about the rise and fall, their height off the canvas, the spaces they leave in between stitches. This is your invitation to experiment. Slanted elongated brick might be the perfect stitch for capturing a flowing hairstyle, but for creating the pitted skin of a lemon, could there be a better stitch than the variation of criss-cross Hungarian stitch? Well, that will depend on *your* imagination!

Life's a beach

I'd like to share with you my design process when I was creating my desert-island idyll for the Beside the Sea Beach Bag. I decided I wanted a realistic rendition of waves lapping on the shoreline to draw the eye into my scene. So I needed movement and depth in my choice, and it had to allow me to play with different colour tones as the sea hits the sand. All this from just one stitch!

Once I had this in mind, I started to think about the stitches that might work. Mini wave stitch could look sweet, but then again a stitch worked on the diagonal would really accentuate the flow of the water. The Bargello wave stitch was just the ticket! But a stitch's relationship with its neighbour is important, too. For my sandy beach, I didn't want another diagonally worked stitch distracting from the flow of the water, so I had to find a horizontally or vertically worked stitch to give me contrast. Sandhills stitch became an obvious choice. What a dream stitch pair!

Always take the time to assess the design to get familiar with the areas you have to fill. I find very often that when you're looking for stitches, it helps to break down your search to areas where you'd like to add movement or spaces where you want to add texture, whether for a specific purpose (like the lemon skin!), or to just shift the perspective on an abstract shape.

DETAIL OF WAVE BREAKING ONTO SAND FROM BESIDE THE SEA BEACH BAG.

REMEMBER THE OLD ADAGE, LESS IS MORE! SOMETIMES YOU CAN WORK WONDERS BY JUST ADDING IN A COUPLE OF DECORATIVE STITCH CHOICES.

BASICS

These three basics are the start point for most stitchers as they begin their needlepoint journey. All members of the tent stitch family, they may look the same from the top but they work their way in and out of the canvas in slightly different ways. These must-know stitches are a perfect go-to to fill in any area of canvas. When worked solely on their own, they'll reward you with a lovely relaxing stitching experience, as your muscle memory kicks in and you switch into auto-stitch mode.

TENT STITCH

Sometimes referred to as a half cross stitch, this small diagonal stitch covers a single canvas intersection and is the essential needlepoint stitch. Fill large areas neatly by working in rows.

- Working from left to right, bring the needle up at 1 and down through the canvas hole at 2.
- Bring the needle back up at 3 and down at 4.
- Continue in this way until you have a row filling the desired width.
- Starting the next row working from right to left, bring the needle up at 9, down at 10, up at 11 and down at 12, and continue to the end of the row.

Start each new row working in the opposite direction from the one before it.

CONTINENTAL STITCH

The continental stitch looks the same as tent stitch from the front, but has a lot more going on underneath! Worked in the opposite direction, it requires more yarn but is more hard wearing.

- Working from right to left, bring the needle up at 1 and down through the canvas hole at 2.
- Bring the needle back up at 3 and down at 4.
- Continue in this way until you have a row filling the desired width.
- Starting the next row working from left to right, bring the needle up at 11, down at 12, up at 13 and down at 14, and continue to the end of the row.

Start each new row working in the opposite direction from the one before it.

If you turn your stitching over, you will see long slanted stitches on the reverse, which provides more coverage, making this stitch ideal for projects subject to wear and tear.

BASKETWEAVE STITCH

Basketweave stitch looks similar to tent and continental stitch from the front, but is worked in diagonal rows up and down the canvas.

Basketweave is best for covering large areas, as it causes the least distortion to the canvas.

- Bring the needle up at 1 and down through the canvas hole at 2.
- Dropping down below the first stitch, now work diagonally across the canvas. Bring the needle back up at 3 and down at 4, then up at 5 and down at 6.
- Bring the needle up at 7, down at 8, up at 9, and so on, to work the next row of stitches diagonally.
- Continue in this way until you have filled the desired area.

MOVEMENT

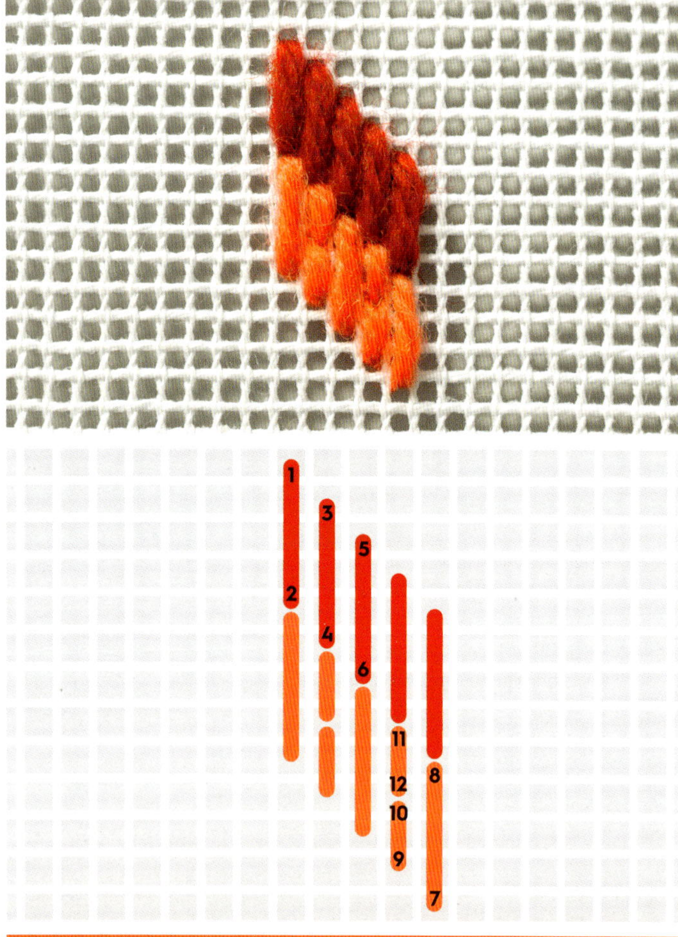

ALBEMARLE STITCH

As all the parts of this stitch are worked vertically it's super easy to compensate. But don't let its straight lengths fool you – this stitch is all about the illusion of movement.

- Working from left to right, bring the needle up at 1 and down through the canvas hole at 2, across four bars of canvas. Bring the needle up at 3 and down at 4, up at 5 and down at 6, and continue until the gently sloping column of stitches fills your desired width.
- To complete the second part of the stitch, bring the needle up at 7 and down through the canvas hole at 8, across four bars of canvas. Then bring the needle up at 9 and down at 10, this time across only two bars of canvas, and up at 11 and down 12, again across two bars of canvas. Continue in this way to complete the row.

Changing colours to work the first and second part of this stitch really highlights its different sections.

ELONGATED CASHMERE STEPS

The lovely structured movement of this stitch makes it ideal for working roof tiles, garden paths and brickwork.

- Working from top to bottom, bring the needle up at 1 and down through the canvas hole at 2, across one intersection of canvas.
- Bring the needle back up at 3 and down at 4, across two intersections of canvas, and repeat to work a total of four stitches in parallel.
- To complete your first block of elongated cashmere, bring the needle up at 11 and down at 12, across just one intersection of canvas.

Now, to create the step, we're going to work the same block just tilted in a different direction.

- Working from right to left, bring the needle up at 13 and down at 14, across one intersection of canvas. Bring the needle up at 15 and down at 16, across two intersections, and repeat to work a total of four stitches in parallel. Bring the needle up at 23 and down at 24, across one intersection of canvas, to complete the block.

Repeat these vertical and horizontal blocks of elongated cashmere steps to fill your canvas.

JACQUARD STITCH

If you're looking for a stepped stitch with a bit more impact, look no further!

- Working from bottom to top, bring the needle up at 1 and down through the canvas hole at 2, going across one intersection of canvas. Then up at 3 and down at 4, again across one intersection. Repeat until you have nine small diagonal stitches worked one directly above the other, then work four stitches in a horizontal row to the left, up at 5 and down at 6, up at 7 and down at 8, up at 9 and down at 10, up at 11 and down at 12.
- Continue in this way until you've filled the height of your canvas area.

Now to work a band of wider diagonal stitches. This has most impact when worked in a second colour.

- Working from bottom to top, bring the needle up at 13 and down through the canvas hole at 14, across three intersections of canvas, up at 15 and down at 16, and continue to stitch a long diagonal stitch alongside each of the small stitches.

Repeat to stitch narrow and wide columns of diagonal stitches to continue the pattern across the canvas.

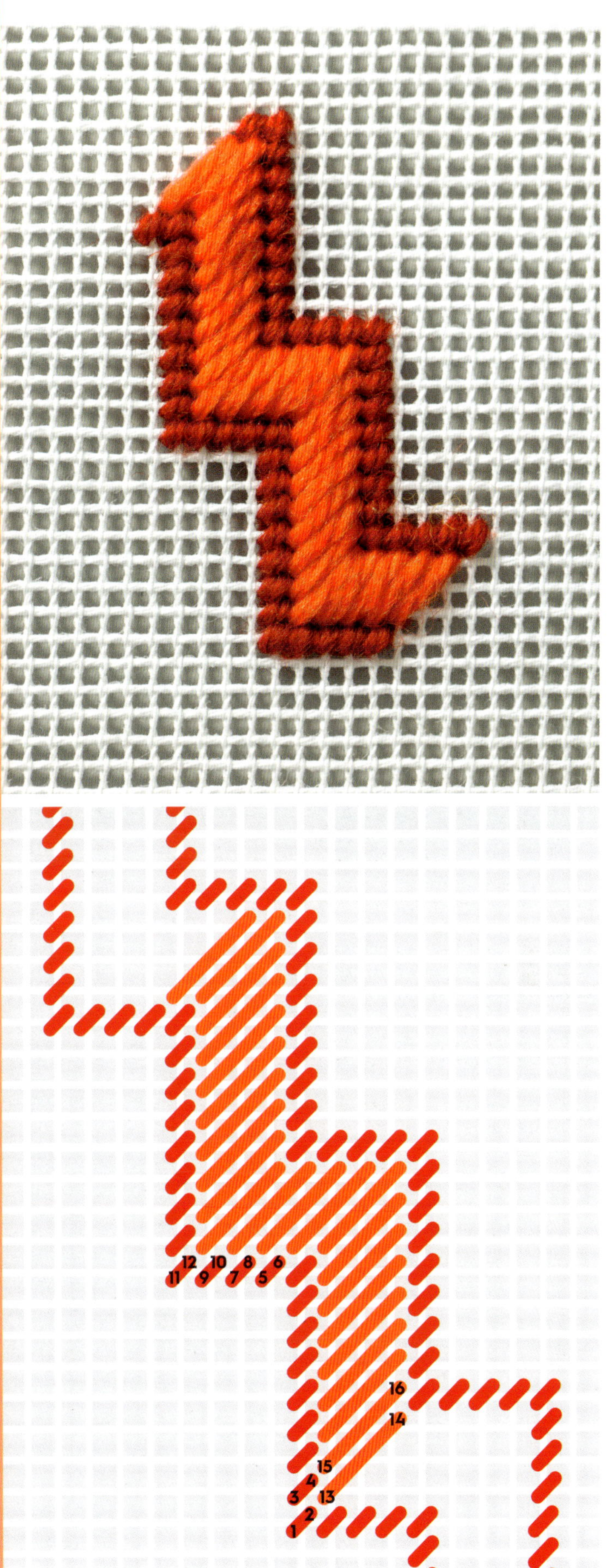

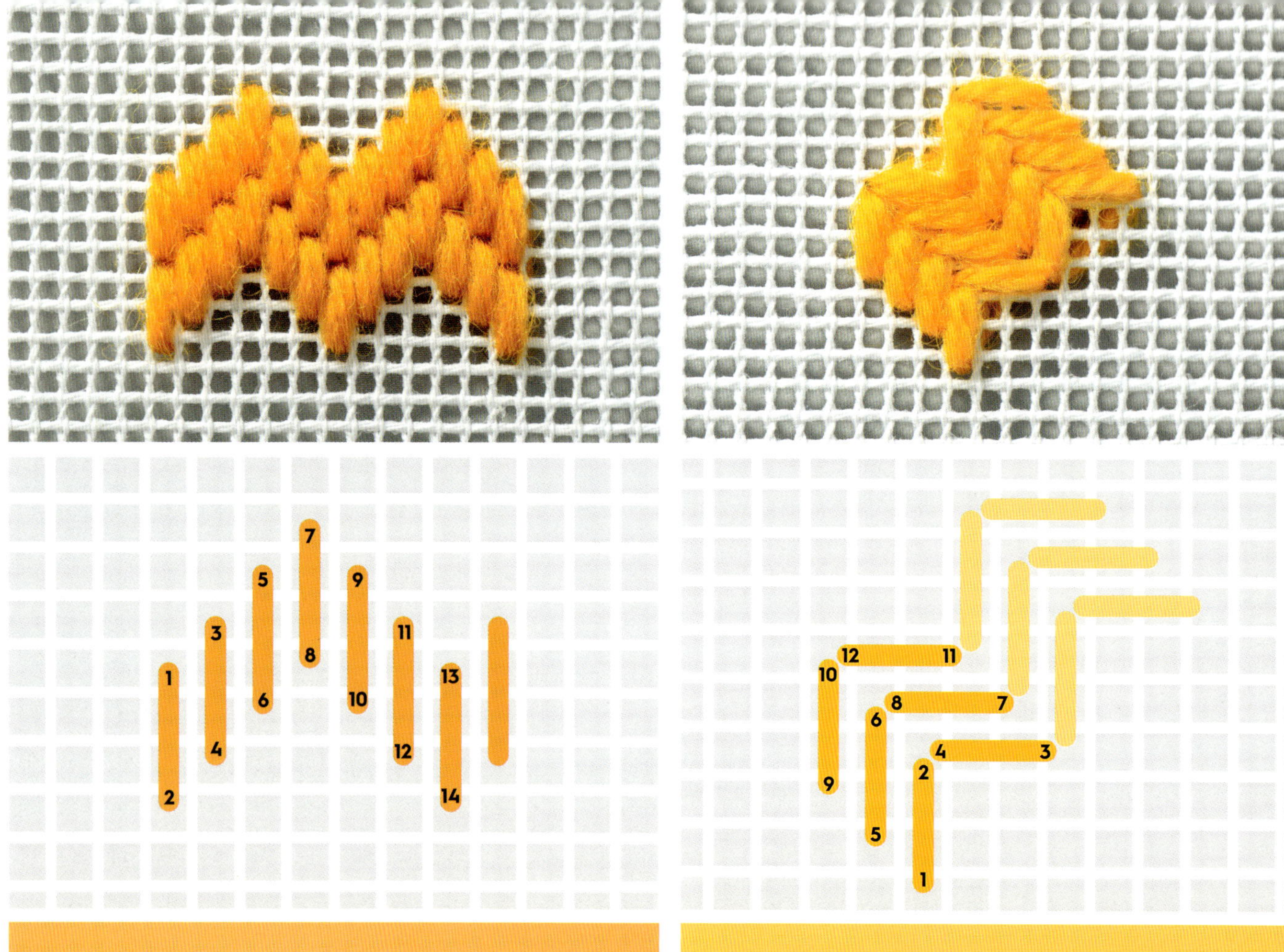

CHEVRON STITCH

Needlepointers often use this stitch in Bargello projects, as it lends itself well to creating waves of different colours to build eye-catching designs.

- Working from left to right, bring the needle up at 1 and down through the canvas hole at 2, going across three bars of canvas.
- Continuing to work across three bars of canvas, bring the needle up at 3 and down at 4, up at 5 and down at 6, up at 7 and down at 8, up at 9 and down at 10, up at 11 and down at 12, up at 13 and down at 14.
- Continue in this way until you have a row of chevrons filling the desired width.
- Building up the chevron pattern one row at a time, work the next row directly beneath the one above, lining up the stitches neatly.

DAMASK STITCH

This may look like a difficult stitch to compensate but, worked in straight lines, it's incredibly easy to work into tricky areas, making it useful for backgrounds; however, I love using it for feathers best!

- Working from bottom to top, bring the needle up at 1 and down through the canvas hole at 2, across three bars of canvas. Bring the needle up at 3 and down at 4, again across three bars of canvas, to form a right angle.
- Bring the needle up at 5 and down at 6, then up at 7 and down at 8, to make a second right-angled stitch, and continue in this way to create a diagonal row of this dynamic stitch shape with each stitch a step above the last.
- Work the next diagonal row alongside the first, lining up the starting points as shown in the diagram.

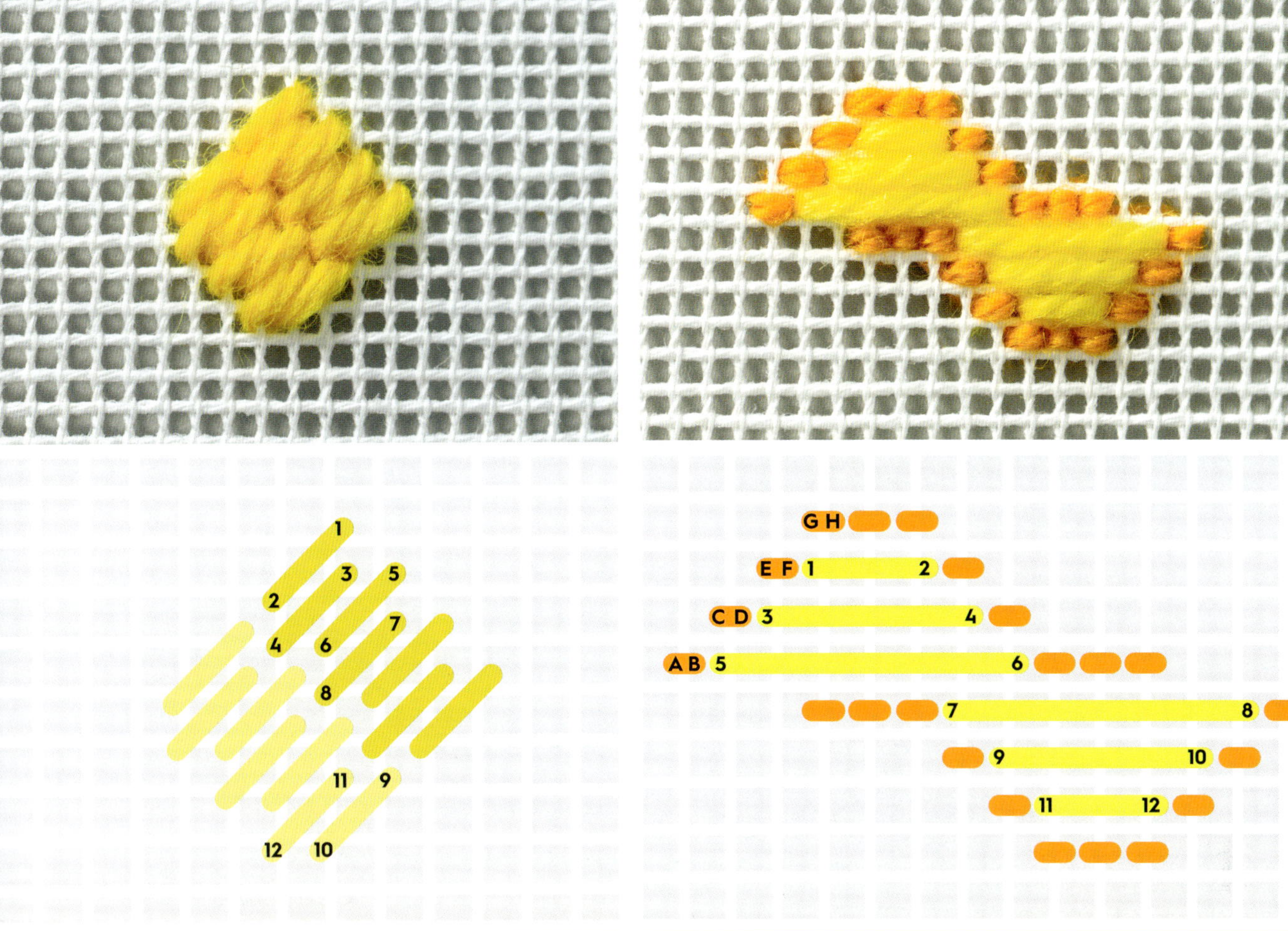

STAGGERED DIAGONAL STITCH

The simple ripple of this stitch makes it a great choice for capturing movement on a body of water.

- Working from top to bottom, bring the needle up at 1 and down through the canvas hole at 2, across two intersections of canvas. Bring the needle up at 3 and down at 4, again across two intersections of canvas to complete your first diagonal.
- Bring the needle up at 5 and down at 6, up at 7 and down at 8, each across two intersections of canvas to complete your first diagonal stagger.
- Continue to stitch pairs of diagonals in this way, stepping down each time as shown in the diagram.
- Starting your next column from bottom to top, bring the needle up at 9 and down at 10, up at 11 and down at 12, and continue to work pairs of diagonal stitches alongside those in the previous column.

HORIZONTAL MILANESE STITCH VARIATION

With its triangular shaping, this stitch is perfect when you want to add some bold movement to your projects.

- Working from left to right, bring the needle up at 1 and down through the canvas hole at 2, across three bars of canvas, up at 3 and down at 4, across five bars, up at 5 and down at 6, across seven bars.
- Stitch a mirror image of this block of stitches staggered to the side, starting by bringing your needle up at 7 and down at 8.
- Continue in this way to stitch mirroring blocks of stitches until you have filled your desired width.

Now to outline the blocks with the smaller stitches.

- Bring your needle up at A and down at B, across one bar of canvas, up at C and down at D, up at E and down at F, up at G and down at H, and so on to complete the line of stitches as shown on the diagram, mirroring this on the block beneath too.

BIRDS AND BLOSSOMS BANNER

STAGGERED HALF DIAMOND RAY STITCH MEETS THE APTLY NAMED WING STITCH TO RAISE YOUR BIRDS INTO FLIGHT. THIS PROJECT IS A CELEBRATION OF MOVEMENT STITCHES SHOWCASED ON AN EASY-TO-FINISH BANNER. REFER TO THE MAKING UP SECTION FOR THE INSTRUCTIONS AND CHARTS FOR THIS PROJECT.

STAGGERED HALF DIAMOND RAY STITCH

This beautiful stitch works so well to give the appearance of ruffled feathers. There are a lot of shared canvas holes in this one, so you need to approach it carefully.

+ Working from right to left, bring the needle up at 1 and down through the canvas hole at 2, across four bars of canvas. Locate the hole diagonally above 1 and bring the needle up at 3 and down at 2, then find the hole diagonally above 3 and bring the needle up at 4 and down at 2.

You have now completed your first half diamond ray stitch. To introduce the stagger, it is important to carefully place the starting point of your next stitch.

+ Find the canvas hole directly below 4 and bring the needle up at 5 and down at 6, across four bars of canvas. Continue as before.

WING STITCH

This is another of my go-to stitches for feathers, this time worked in a more open way with each completed wing stitch sitting alongside another, perfect for a bird in flight.

This stitch works well in different directions as seen in the Birds and Blossoms Banner, so you could have fun experimenting, turning it 90 degrees at a time.

+ Working from right to left across the row, bring the needle up at 1 and down through the canvas hole at 2, travelling across five bars of canvas in a tilted diagonal.
+ Bring the needle up at 3 and down again at 2, up at 4 and down again at 2, up at 5 and down again at 2, up at 6 and down again at 2 to complete your first wing stitch.

Notice how the start point of each of the diagonal stitches is always two holes away from the start point of the previous stitch, alternately vertically then horizontally.

DIAGONAL GREEK STITCH

Whether you want to stitch fur, grass or roofing, the movement of this stitch could be just what you're looking for!

- Working from left to right, bring the needle up at 1 and down through the canvas hole at 2, across two bars of canvas. Then bring the needle up at 3 and down at 4, across four bars of canvas but stepping up across only one, to create a tilted diagonal.
- Bring the needle up at 5 and down at 6, across two bars of canvas, trapping the end of the first diagonal stitch. Bring the needle up at 7 and down at 8 to create a tilted diagonal as before.
- Continue to work staggered stitches in this way until you have reached the width of your canvas.
- To start the next row, begin stitching two holes below 1 using a new thread, and continue as before.

DIAGONAL PAIRS

With its tight zigzag motion, this stitch is excellent worked in multiple shades of green for trees, or in a variety of whites for clouds.

- Working from left to right, bring the needle up at 1 and down through the canvas hole at 2, going across two intersections of canvas. Bring the needle up at 3 and down at 4, again over two intersections, to create a parallel diagonal stitch to the first.
- Bring the needle up at 5 (two holes along from the start of your previous stitch) and down through the canvas hole at 6, going across two intersections. Bring the needle up at 7 and down at 8 to complete the second diagonal pair of stitches.
- Continue to work staggered pairs of diagonal stitches in this way until you have reached your desired height and width.
- Starting the next row from right to left, change the direction of your diagonal pairs as shown in the diagram (9 and 10, 11 and 12).

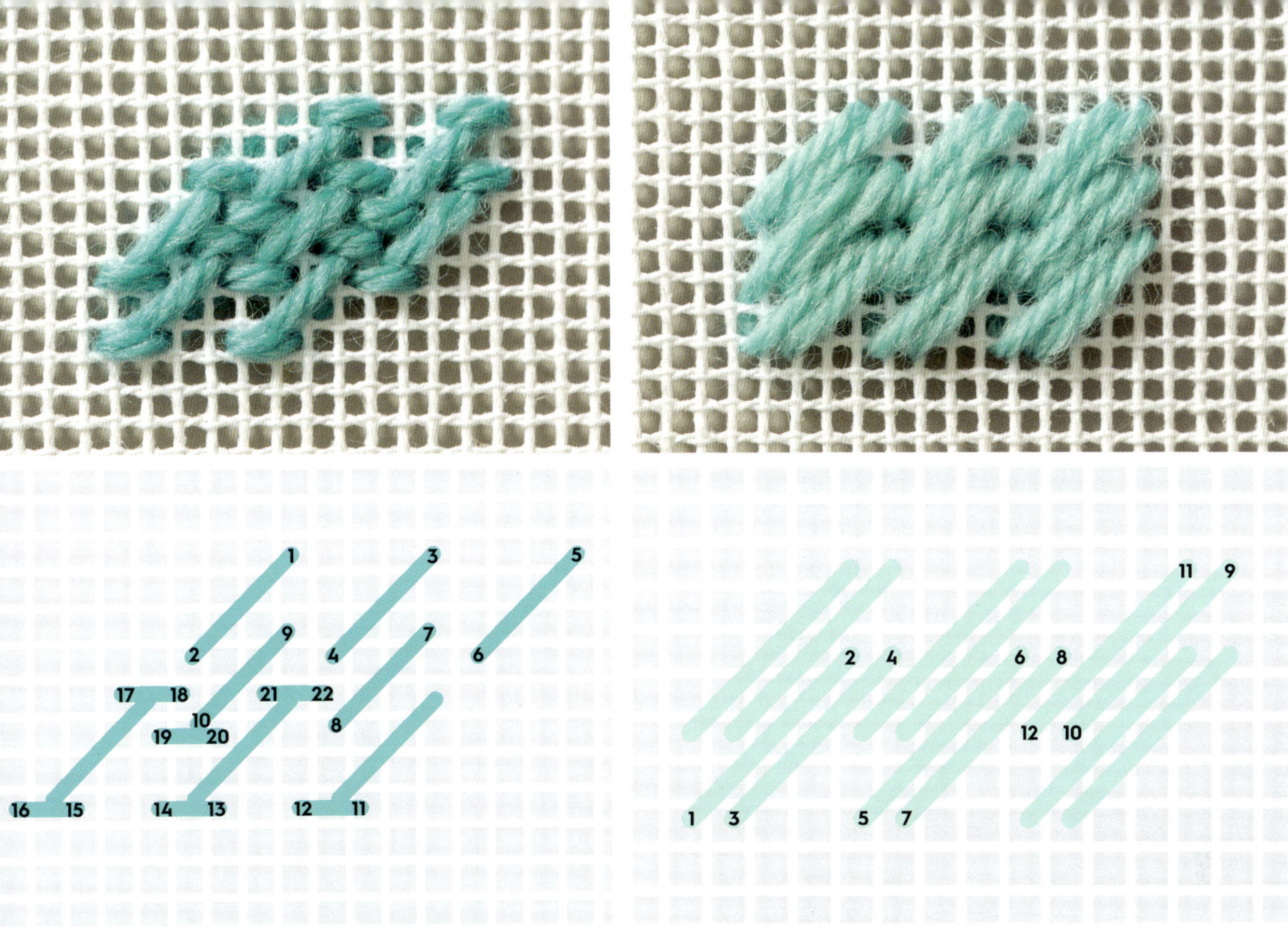

ITALIC STITCH

I like to approach this stitch by completing all the long diagonals first before capping them with the shorter horizontal stitches.

- Working from left to right, bring the needle up at 1 and down through the canvas hole at 2, across three intersections of canvas. Bring the needle up at 3 (four bars over to the right) and down at 4, and continue until you have filled the desired width.
- Working the next row from right to left, bring the needle up at 7 and down at 8, up at 9 and down at 10, so that this row of stitches is staggered two holes below the first row.

Once you have filled your desired area with your diagonal stitches, it's time to add your horizontal stitches.

- Bring the needle up at 11 and down at 12, across two bars of canvas, and continue in this way to work a vertical stitch at each end of your diagonal stitches (the diagram shows this in progress).

SLANTED ELONGATED DOUBLE BRICK STITCH

I absolutely adore using this stitch for hair. It gives you good smooth lengths but with a gorgeous rippled effect.

- Working from left to right, bring the needle up at 1 and down through the canvas hole at 2, across four intersections of canvas. Then bring the needle up at 3 and down at 4 to create a parallel stitch.
- Leaving a gap of two canvas holes, bring the needle up at 5 and down at 6, up at 7 and down at 8. Continue creating pairs of stitches in this way until you have a row filling the desired width.

Start the next row in the opposite direction, so your stitches are staggered between the stitches of your first row.

- Working from right to left, bring the needle up at 9 and down at 10, up at 11 and down at 12, and continue in this way to the end of the row.

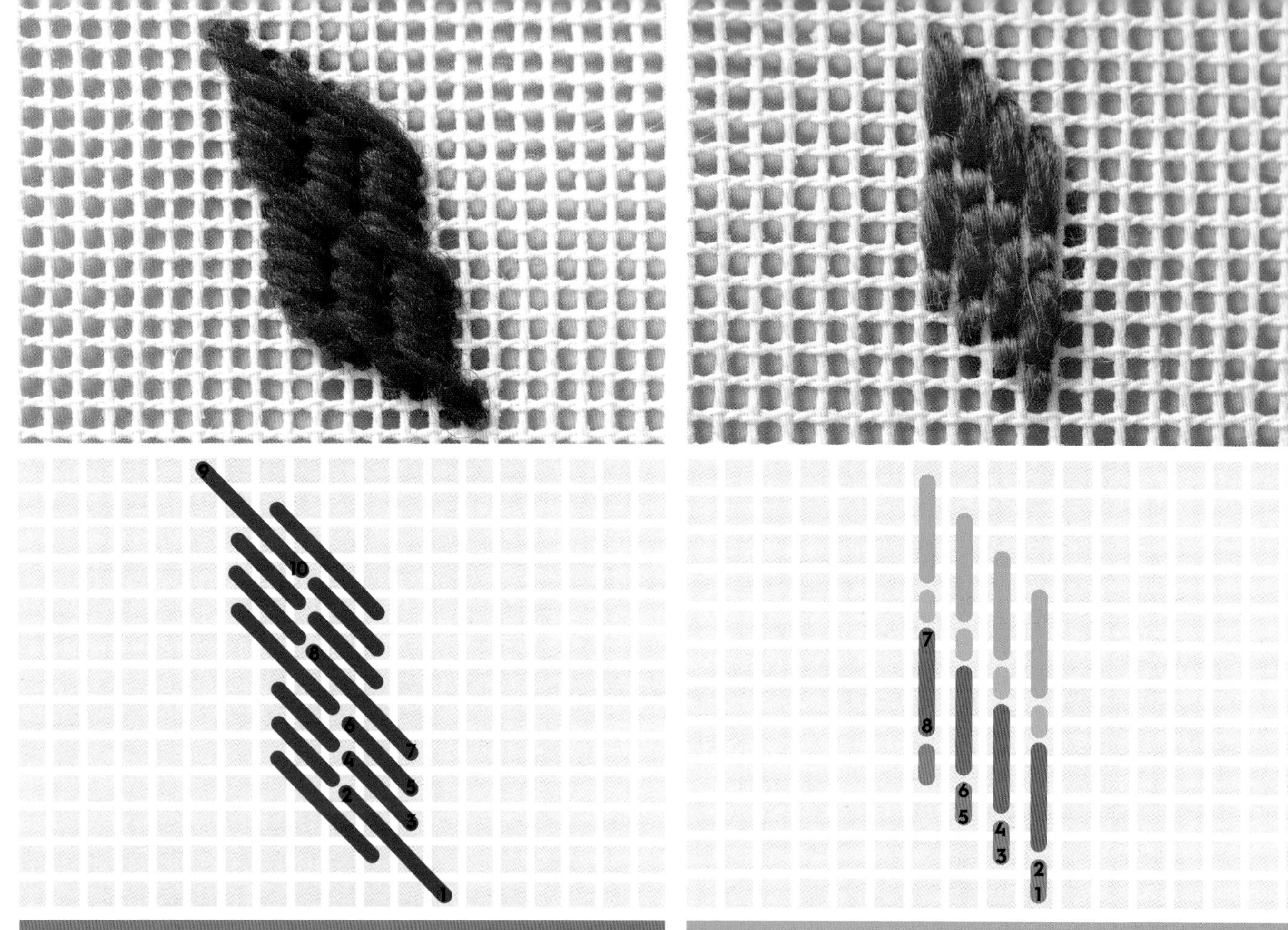

CONDENSED CASHMERE STITCH VARIATION

This variation on condensed cashmere stitch, with its longer sections, maximizes movement across the canvas with its smooth, seamless appearance.

- Starting at the right-hand side and working diagonally from bottom to top, bring the needle up at 1 and down through the canvas hole at 2, across three intersections of canvas. Bring the needle up at 3 and down at 4, up at 5 and down at 6, across two intersections of canvas. Then bring the needle up at 7 and down at 8, across three intersections, to complete the starting block.

The final stitch of the starting block, 7 to 8, becomes the first stitch of your next block.

- Continue in this way until you have a diagonal row filling the desired height.
- Working the next row in the opposite direction, from bottom to top, bring the needle up at 9 and down at 10, continuing as before to create another column of stitches.

DOUBLE WOVEN STITCH

If you are looking for a quick to work stitch that has an incredible sense of movement, this fits the bill. Worked only with rows of straight vertical stitches, it's ideal for filling large areas of canvas.

- Working from bottom to top, bring the needle up at 1 and down through the canvas hole at 2, across one bar of canvas. Bring the needle up at 3 and down at 4, up at 5 and down at 6, each across one bar of canvas, a step up from the last stitch each time. Continue in this way until you have filled your desired width.
- Working the next row from bottom to top, bring the needle up at 7 and down at 8, across three bars of canvas, and continue along the row so that each single-bar straight stitch is topped with a long three-bar straight stitch.
- Continue to repeat the short and long straight stitch rows until you have filled your desired height.

SWEET AND SIMPLE CAKE FLAGS

THESE LITTLE CAKE FLAGS ARE A GREAT WAY TO PRACTISE NEW STITCHES. I'VE CHOSEN FOUR OF MY FAVOURITES INCLUDING DOUBLE WOVEN STITCH AND CONDENSED CASHMERE STITCH VARIATION, BUT WHICH WILL YOU CHOOSE? REFER TO THE MAKING UP SECTION FOR THE INSTRUCTIONS AND CHART FOR THIS PROJECT.

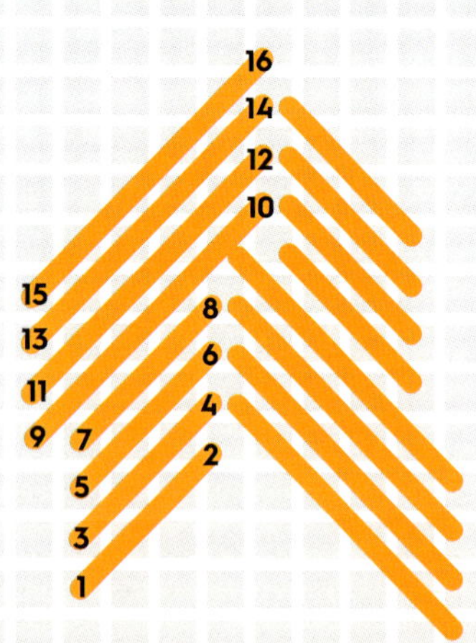

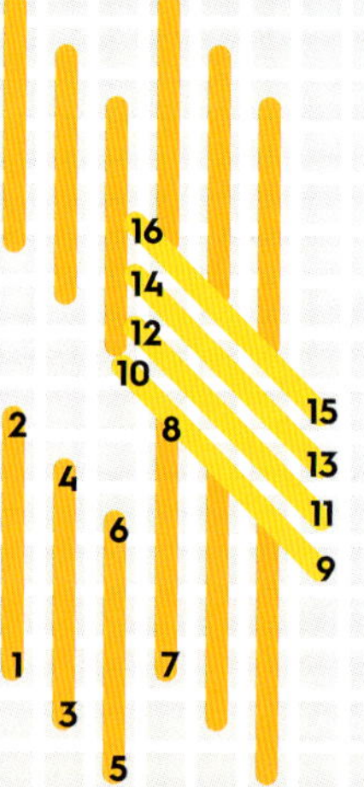

QUADRUPLE ALTERNATING NOBUKO

This is a really bold stitch that travels across a lot of intersections, so you need a big area to really let it shine.

- Working from bottom to top, bring the needle up at 1 and down through the canvas hole at 2, across three intersections of canvas. Then bring the needle up at 3 and down at 4, up at 5 and down at 6, up at 7 and down at 8 to complete a set of four parallel diagonal stitches, one above the other.

Now work a block of four long diagonal stitches above, as follows:

- Bring the needle up at 9 and down at 10, across five intersections of canvas. Complete three more parallel stitches (11 to 12, 13 to 14, 15 to 16).
- Continue in this way, alternating short stitch blocks with long stitch blocks, until you reach the desired height.
- Working the next column from top to bottom with stitches facing in the opposite direction, and starting one bar above for a staggered effect, alternate long stitch blocks with short stitch blocks as seen in the diagram.

RUSSELL VARIANT STITCH

This is lovely bold movement stitch but it requires a few stitch tucks as you go.

- Working from bottom to top and left to right, bring the needle up at 1 and down through the canvas hole at 2, across five bars of canvas. Bring the needle up at 3 and down at 4, up at 5 and down at 6, , as seen in the diagram.
- Bring the needle up at 7 and down at 8, and continue to stitch sets of three stitches in this way until you have a row to your desired width.

For the next row, we'll be working a set of four diagonal stitches above each set of three vertical stitches on the previous row, as seen in the stitched sample (for clarity, only one set is shown in the diagram).

- Bring the needle up at 9 and down through the canvas hole at 10, going across four intersections of canvas, up at 11 and down at 12, up at 13 and down at 14, up at 15 and down at 16.

As you start to build up these stitches row by row and column by column your threads will overlap some stitch ends; just gently tuck your needle underneath.

DIAGONAL BEATY STITCH

Worked in bands, this interlocking stitch will give you a structured sense of movement that's really fun to play with.

- Working from left to right, bring the needle up at 1 and down through the canvas hole at 2, across two intersections of canvas. Then bring the needle up at 3 and down at 4, again across two intersections to create a pair of diagonal stitches.
- For the second pair of diagonal stitches, bring the needle up at 5 and down at 6, across three intersections of canvas, then up at 7 and down at 8.
- Continue to repeat these two pairs of diagonal stitches until you fill the desired width.
- For the next row, working from right to left, make pairs of the short stitches opposite the long stitches and vice versa.

STEPPED BRICK STITCH

I adore this stitch. It's amazing worked in a single colour, highly impactful in multiple colours, and just dreamy for an ombre effect.

- Working each diagonal row in turn, from bottom right to top left, bring the needle up at 1 and down through the canvas hole at 2, across six bars of canvas.
- Bring the needle up at 3 and down at 4, across two bars of canvas, and repeat to work a total of six small straight stitches, each stepping up one bar each time.
- To complete the row, bring the needle up at 7 and down at 8, across six bars of canvas.

You can keep extending the row upwards, using 7 and 8 as the starting point for the next run of six small straight stitches, but here, I'm showing how to sit the rows of stitches one on top of the other.

- To start the next row, bring the needle up at 9 and down at 10, across six bars of canvas. Then up at 11 and down at 12, across two bars of canvas, and continue as before.

ESCALATORS

This stitch is on the move all the way – stitch it 'open' as shown here, or for a more dramatic look, fill in the gap with a secondary colour, or even a metallic!

+ Working from left to right, bring the needle up at 1 and down through the canvas hole at 2, across four bars of canvas. Bring the needle up at 3 and down at 4, up at 5 and down at 6, up at 7 and down at 8 for a total of four parallel stitches.
+ Bring the needle up at 9 and down at 10, across four bars of canvas, but this time stepping up one hole. Create three more stepped stitches (11 to 12, 13 to 14, 15 to 16) to complete the first escalator stitch.
+ Continue in this way until you have filled the desired height, and when you're ready to start your next row, head back down, starting with 17 to 18.

WIDE STEPS

This open stitch is ideally worked onto a coloured canvas. The route I take uses up a lot of thread, but it's worth it, as it produces a really neat finish.

+ Working from left to right, bring the needle up at 1 and down through the canvas hole at 2, across two intersections of canvas, then up at 3 and down at 4, and up at 5 and down at 6, and continue until you have filled the desired width.
+ Bring the needle up at 7 and down at 8, across four bars of canvas, then up at 9 and down at 10, up at 11 and down at 12, and continue until you have filled the desired width.
+ Continue in this way until you have filled the desired area.

SNAZZY SNEEZERS TISSUE BOX

THIS TISSUE BOX COVER SHOWS OFF THE PSYCHEDELIC MOVEMENT STITCH IN ALL ITS GLORY, USING FIVE COLOURS TO BUILD UP ITS BEAUTIFUL DESIGN. REFER TO THE MAKING UP SECTION FOR THE INSTRUCTIONS AND CHART FOR THIS PROJECT.

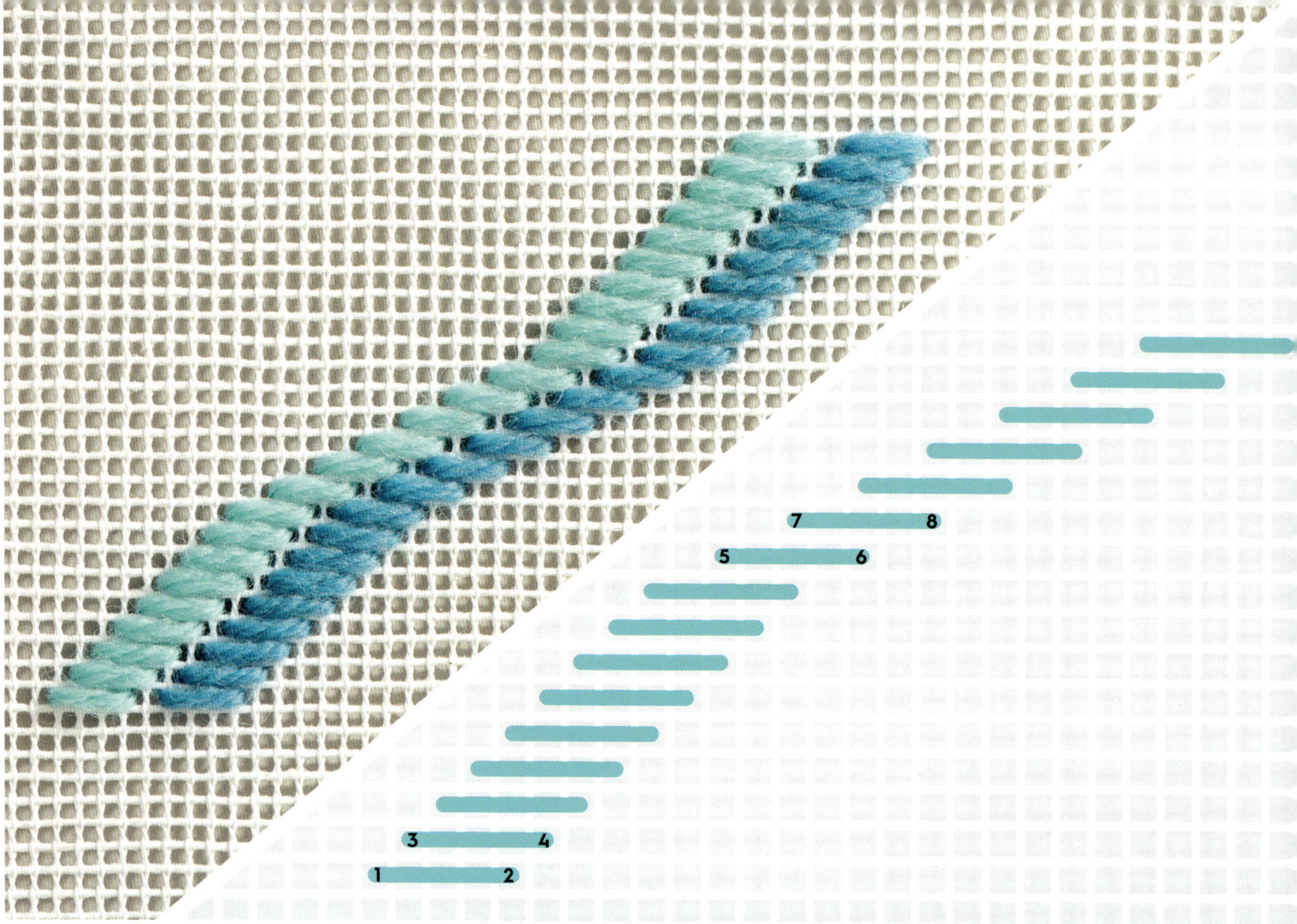

MOVEMENT STITCH

Simple yet effective, the perfectly named movement stitch brings a sense of dynamism to a design, and the more colours you use, the groovier the pattern will be.

- Working from bottom to top, bring the needle up at 1 and down through the canvas hole at 2, going across four bars of canvas. Bring the needle up at 3 and down at 4, again across four bars of canvas, this time stepping one hole to the right. Repeat to stitch a total of nine stitches.
- Now taking a two hole step to the right, bring the needle up at 5 and down at 6, across four bars of canvas. Repeat to stitch a total of seven stitches like this. Continue in this way until you have a column filling the desired height.

TOP TIPS FOR STITCH SELECTION

YOU HAVE A FRESH NEW NEEDLEPOINT CANVAS IN FRONT OF YOU, WHERE DO YOU START? HERE ARE A FEW OF MY TOP TIPS TO HELP YOU ON YOUR WAY...

TIP #1: START SIMPLY

IF YOU'RE RELATIVELY NEW TO WORKING WITH DECORATIVE NEEDLEPOINT STITCHES, YOU MIGHT FIND IT EASIER TO START BY PICKING A PROJECT WITH EASY-TO-STITCH AREAS. DESIGNS WITH CLEAR GRAPHIC LINES, GEOMETRIC SHAPES AND BIG BLOCKS OF COLOUR ARE AN EXCELLENT CHOICE.

TIP #2: STITCH AT THE EDGE

I USE THE EDGE OF MY CANVAS TO TEST OUT LITTLE SWATCHES OF THE STITCHES I'M SHORTLISTING FOR MY DESIGN. IT'S A GREAT WAY TO SEE HOW DIFFERENT STITCHES WILL LOOK ALONGSIDE EACH OTHER BEFORE YOU COMMIT THEM TO THE BODY OF THE CANVAS.

TIP #3: QUESTION YOUR CHOICES

IMAGINE A DESIGN MADE UP OF LOTS OF GEOMETRIC COLOUR BLOCKS. WOULD YOU WANT THE STITCHES OF NEIGHBOURING BLOCKS TO ALL BE WORKED ON VERTICALS? PROBABLY NOT. IN THE INTERESTS OF CONTRAST, MIGHT A DIAGONALLY WORKED STITCH SIT BETTER ALONGSIDE AN AREA WORKED VERTICALLY? ASK YOURSELF QUESTIONS LIKE THESE BEFORE YOU MAKE A START.

TIP #4: PLOT YOUR ROUTE

I FIND IT REALLY HELPFUL TO SPEND A LITTLE TIME PLOTTING MY WAY AROUND MY CANVAS, CHECKING OUT THOSE AREAS THAT OVERLAP. IN THIS WAY, I CAN MAKE SURE THAT I DON'T UNINTENTIONALLY ADD TOO MUCH CONTRAST. I ALWAYS HAVE A LITTLE NOTEBOOK ON HAND TO SCRIBBLE DOWN MY STITCH IDEAS, AND I CAN'T RECOMMEND THIS HIGHLY ENOUGH.

TIP #5: BUILD YOUR SKILLS

WHY NOT CREATE YOUR OWN REFERENCE SAMPLER? TAKE A PIECE OF BLANK CANVAS AND MARK OUT SOME SQUARES TO FILL WITH DECORATIVE STITCHES. IT'S A GREAT WAY TO DISCOVER YOUR PERSONAL FAVOURITES.

PICK A PROJECT WITH EASY-TO-STITCH AREAS.

BUILD YOUR SKILLS BY PRACTISING SINGLE STITCHES.

TEXTURE

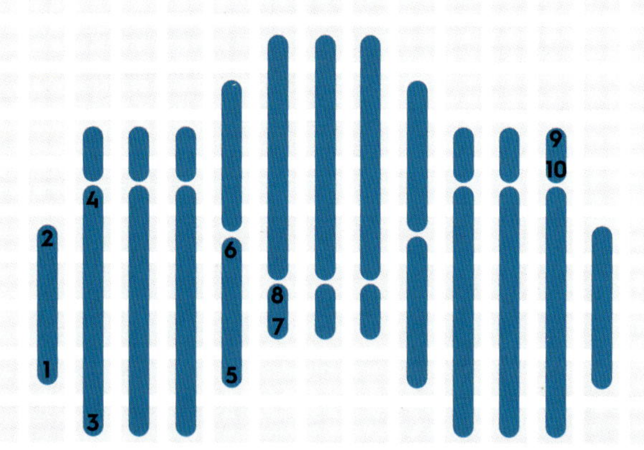

BALLOON STITCH

This stitch is created with just easy straight stitches, yet it makes a beautiful curved texture that is excellent for backgrounds.

- Working from left to right, bring the needle up at 1 and down through the canvas hole at 2, across three bars of canvas.
- Bring the needle up at 3 and down at 4, across five bars of canvas, and stitch two more identical stitches. Then bring the needle up at 5 and down at 6, across three bars of canvas to complete your first balloon stitch.

The balloon stitches are connected to each other by a series of three single-bar straight stitches.

- Bring the needle up at 7 and down at 8, across one bar of canvas, and repeat two more times.
- You are now ready to start your next balloon stitch. Continue in this way until you have a row filling the desired width.
- When you start your next row (9 to 10), make sure that the short single-bar stitches sit perfectly above the long five-bar stitches in the row below.

This example was worked in rows from bottom to top, but could just as easily be stitched from top to bottom.

BALLOON STITCH VARIATION

You can add a different texture to a canvas with the smallest of changes. Look how balloon stitch is transformed by flipping direction and taking out the connecting stitches.

- Working from bottom to top, bring the needle up at 1 and down through the canvas hole at 2, across four bars of canvas.
- Bring the needle up at 3 and down at 4, across six bars of canvas, and stitch two more identical stitches. Then bring the needle up at 5 and down at 6, across four bars of canvas to complete your first balloon stitch variation.
- To start your next stitch, skip the next row of holes to bring the needle up at 7 and down at 8 and continue as before.
- To begin a new column, work your balloon stitches from top to bottom, making sure to stagger them so the shorter stitches line up alongside the longer stitches and vice versa, as shown in the diagram.

BUBBLE STITCH

Perfect for larger areas, working in two colours to showcase the stitch lengths.

- Working from left to right, bring the needle up at 1 and down through the canvas hole at 2, across one intersection of canvas. Then up at 3 and down at 4, up at 5 and down at 6, up at 7 and down at 8. This creates the little square of tent stitches that separates your bubble stitches.
- To stitch the first half of the bubble, bring the needle up at 9 and down at 10, across three intersections of canvas, up at 11 and down at 12, across four intersections, up at 13 and down at 14, across five intersections.
- At the middle of the bubble, bring the needle up at 15 and down at 16, across one intersection of canvas, up at 17 and down at 18, across two intersections, then up at 19 and down at 20, across one intersection.
- To complete the second half of the bubble, mirror the first half, as shown in the diagram. Continue in this way until you have a row filling the desired width.
- On the next row, tilt the bubbles in the opposite direction but continue to stitch the tent stitch blocks facing the same way.

SPLIT SCOTCH STITCH

My love of split stitches started with this stitch. It amazes me the impact that little dimple in the middle has on the texture of your canvas!

- Working from top to bottom, bring the needle up at 1 and down through the canvas hole at 2, across one intersection of canvas. Bring the needle up at 3 and down at 4, across two intersections, and up at 5 and down at 6, across three intersections.
- Now to create that dimple. Bring the needle up at 7 and down at 8, across two intersections of canvas, then up at 9 and down at 10.
- To finish your split Scotch stitch, simply mirror your first three stitches to form a square as shown in the diagram.
- To work the next split Scotch stitch block, bring the needle up at 17 and down at 18, so that the starting stitch sits alongside the middle section of the previous block.

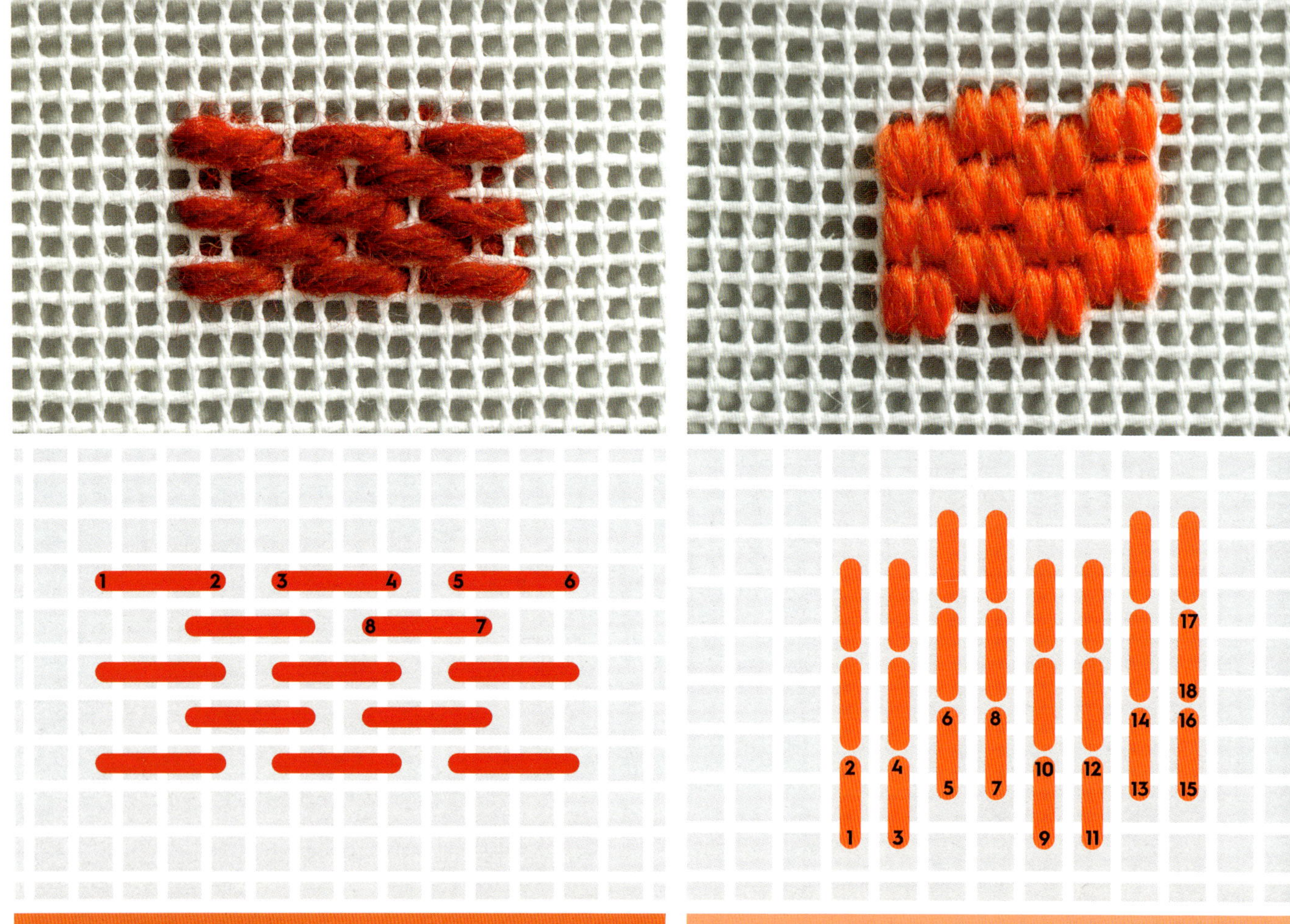

DARNING STITCH

This is an easy-to-learn stitch that gives you tons of texture with super-quick coverage. I love using it for landscape horizons.

- Working from left to right, bring the needle up at 1 and down through the canvas hole at 2, across three bars of canvas. Then skip a bar and bring the needle up at 3 and down at 4. Continue until you have reached the edge of your desired area.
- When you're ready to start your next row, work from right to left and make sure the stitches lie in the middle of the row above, as shown in the diagram (7 to 8).

DOUBLE BRICK STITCH

This is one of my go-to background stitches, as it covers quickly and gives such a beautiful texture.

- Working from left to right, bring the needle up at 1 and down through the canvas hole at 2, across two bars of canvas, up at 3 and down at 4, again across two bars of canvas to give you your first pair of stitches.
- For the next pair of stitches, step up one bar to the right and bring the needle up at 5 and down at 6, up at 7 and down at 8, both across two bars of canvas.
- Continue in this way until you have a row filling the desired width.
- For the next row, working from right to left, mirror the working of the stitches in the row beneath, starting by bringing the needle up at 17 and down 18, so that the rows interlock.

TIDY EDGES

ALL THE PROJECTS IN THIS BOOK ARE DESIGNED ON PLASTIC CANVAS TO HELP YOU EXPLORE THE BREADTH OF ITEMS YOU CAN CREATE WITH NEEDLEPOINT. PLASTIC CANVAS HAS AN INCREDIBLE STRUCTURE THAT GIVES YOU SO MUCH FREEDOM TO BUILD, TO CREATE USEFUL 3D ITEMS LIKE THE TRINKET TRAY OR THE TISSUE BOX COVER, WITHOUT THE NEED TO GET THE SEWING MACHINE OUT. AND YOU CAN FINISH PICTURES AT HOME WITHOUT HAVING TO SEND THEM AWAY TO THE PICTURE FRAMER'S!

BUT SOMETIMES THE EXPOSED PLASTIC CANVAS EDGES CAN LOOK A LITTLE DISTRACTING. KNOWING HOW TO EASILY TIDY THEM ON YOUR PROJECTS IS A MUST! I FIND THE SIMPLEST WAY IS TO WHIP OUT A WHIP STITCH, AN ESSENTIAL STITCH FOR ANY NEEDLEPOINTER.

WHIP STITCH IS AN EASY ONE TO LEARN AND YOU CAN USE IT ON THE EDGES OF SINGLE SHEETS OF PLASTIC CANVAS OR TO JOIN TWO PIECES TOGETHER. IT CAN BE WORKED IN ANY DIRECTION ALONG THE EDGE OF YOUR CANVAS. ON THIS OCCASION IT IS BEING WORKED RIGHT TO LEFT. BRING THE NEEDLE UP THROUGH THE CANVAS HOLE AT 1, LOOP IT AROUND THE EDGE OF THE CANVAS AND BRING IT UP AGAIN IN THE NEIGHBOURING CANVAS HOLE AT 2. THEN LOOP IT AROUND THE EDGE OF THE CANVAS AGAIN TO BRING IT UP AT 3. CONTINUE IN THIS WAY, TURNING THE CANVAS AS YOU REACH THE CORNER TO WORK ALONG THE NEXT EDGE. YOU MAY FIND THAT YOU NEED TO ADD TWO WHIP STITCHES PER HOLE TO NEATEN THE CORNERS.

NEATENING YOUR EDGES WITH WHIP STITCH MEANS THEY WILL SEAMLESSLY BLEND INTO THE BACKGROUND, AS ON THE ELEMENTAL COASTERS. HOWEVER, YOU CAN BRING AN EXTRA FLARE TO A PIECE BY WORKING THEM IN A CONTRASTING COLOUR, AS I HAVE ON MY CUTE CARD KEEPER WALLET.

LEARNING WHIP STITCH IS ESSENTIAL.

SUCH NEAT COASTER CORNERS.

PERFECTLY FINISHED EDGES FOR YOUR CARD WALLET.

DRAGONFLY STITCH

A beautiful stitch, whether worked closely together or in isolation and randomly dotted around a canvas background. Stitched here with embroidery thread, the choice of a thinner thread really accentuates its shape.

+ Working from left to right, bring the needle up at 1 and down through the canvas hole at 2, up at 3 and down at 4, to create an elongated cross, forming the dragonfly's wings.
+ Then bring the needle up at 5 and down at 6, across three intersections of canvas, to form the dragonfly's body.

Notice that when working dragonfly stitch in rows, each stitch sits neatly next to the other.

+ To form the next stitch, count three canvas holes along from 1 (the starting stitch of your first dragonfly) to bring the needle up at 7 and down at 8, and continue as before.

ALICIA'S LACE VARIATION

This lovely open stitch, which shows peeks of the canvas underneath, is great for small-to-medium areas of canvas.

+ Bring the needle up at 1 and down through the canvas hole at 2, across two intersections of canvas, up at 3 and down at 4, up at 5 and down at 6, up at 7 and down at 8 to create a little diamond shape.
+ To build up more diamonds just line up the points, until you've filled your desired area.

Once the diamond grid is complete, 'fill' them with a simple straight stitch worked in a different coloured thread.

+ Bring the needle up at A and down at B, going across two bars of canvas. Continue across each of the diamond shapes.

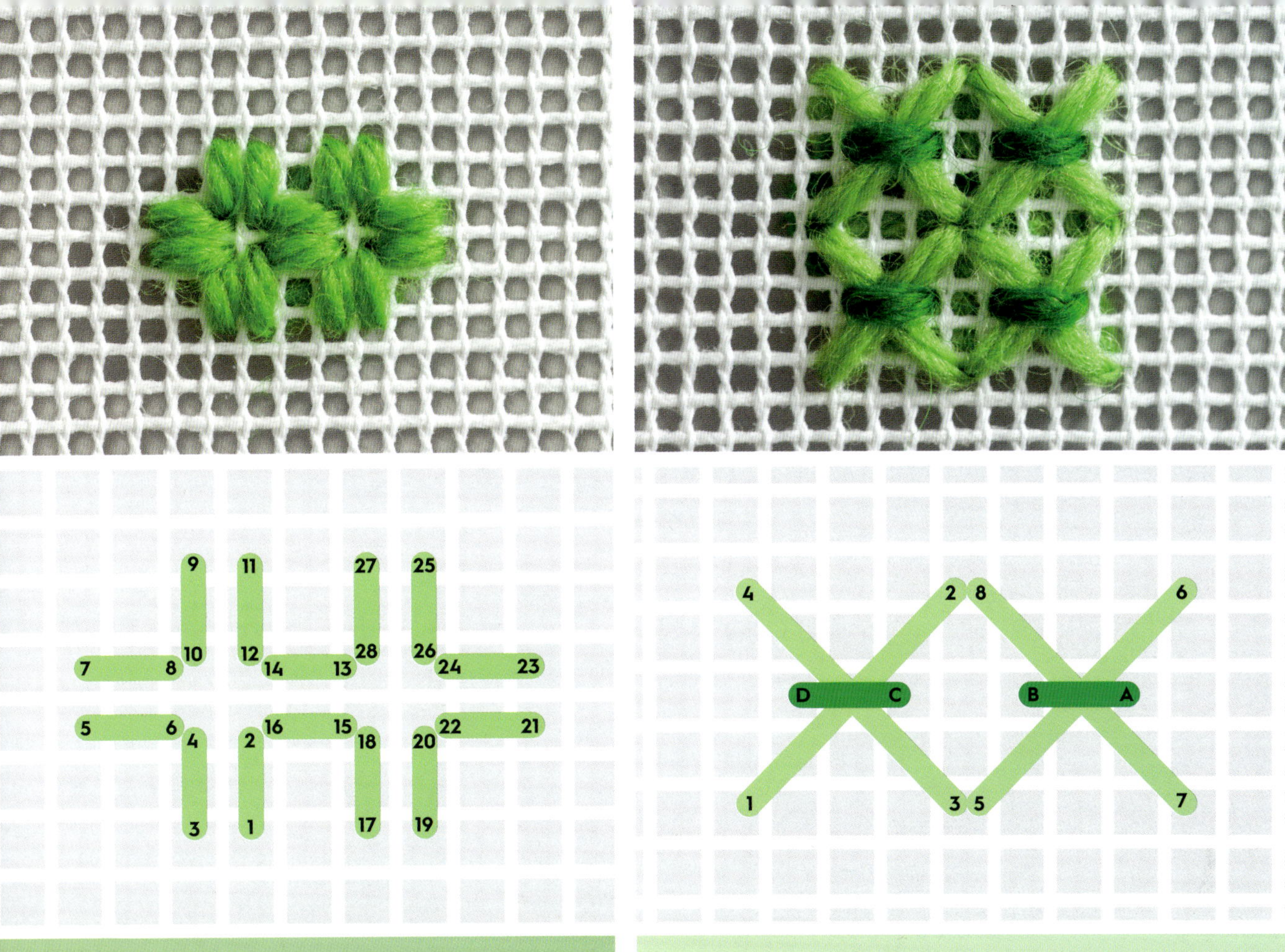

SMALL BROCADE STITCH

This is such a great stitch to add texture to small areas of canvas. It also makes very cute daisies as can be seen on the For Love of Flowers Notebook Cover!

- Bring the needle up at 1 and down through the canvas hole at 2, across two bars of canvas, then up at 3 and down at 4 to create a pair of vertical stitches.
- Moving clockwise, bring the needle up at 5 and down at 6, across two bars of canvas, then up at 7 and down at 8 to create a pair of horizontal stitches.
- Once again moving clockwise, bring the needle up 9 and down at 10, up at 11 and down at 12, and with one more clockwise turn bring your needle up at 13 and down at 14, up at 15 and down at 16 to complete your first small brocade stitch.
- To continue the row, bring the needle up at 17 and down at 18, and notice how as you add your stitches that they share sections, as shown in the diagram.

TACKED LARGE CROSS STITCH

A big, bold texture stitch, this one is best saved for larger areas of canvas to really show it off in all its glory.

- Working from left to right, bring the needle up at 1 and down through the canvas hole at 2, across four intersections of canvas, then up at 3 and down at 4, to complete your first large cross stitch.
- Continue in this way until you have filled your desired area with large cross stitches.

Now to add the tacks to the middle of your crosses.

- Working from right to left, bring the needle up at A and down at B, across two bars of canvas, then up at C and down at D, and continue until each cross has been tacked.

CRISS-CROSS HUNGARIAN STITCH VARIATION

There's a softness to this two-part stitch that I think works particularly well for curly animal fur when working on large sections of canvas.

- Working from left to right, bring the needle up at 1 and down through the canvas hole at 2, across two intersections of canvas. Leaving a gap of two canvas holes between stitches, bring the needle up at 3 and down at 4, and continue like this until you have a row filling the desired width.
- Working from right to left, bring the needle up at 7 and down at 8, across two intersections of canvas, then up at 9 and down at 10, across three intersections, and up at 11 and down at 12, over two intersections to complete a set of three stitches. Continue to work sets of three stitches in this way.

DIAMOND FAN STITCH

Most of the stitches that form the diamond fan stitch share a canvas hole, so using a thinner thread is a good idea. I've used an unstranded length of a stranded cotton (floss) for my sample.

- Bring the needle up at 1 and down through the canvas hole at 2, across three intersections of canvas. Then starting one hole away from the previous stitch each time, bring the needle up at 3 and down at 2, up at 4 and down at 2, up at 5 and down at 2, up at 6 and down at 2, up at 7 and down at 2, up at 8 and down at 2, to create the 'fan'.

Now it's time to frame the fan.

- Bring the needle up at 9 and down at 10, across four intersections of canvas. Continuing to work over four intersections of canvas each time, complete the remaining three sides of the frame following the diagram.

To build up more diamond fans, line them up so the framing points all meet.

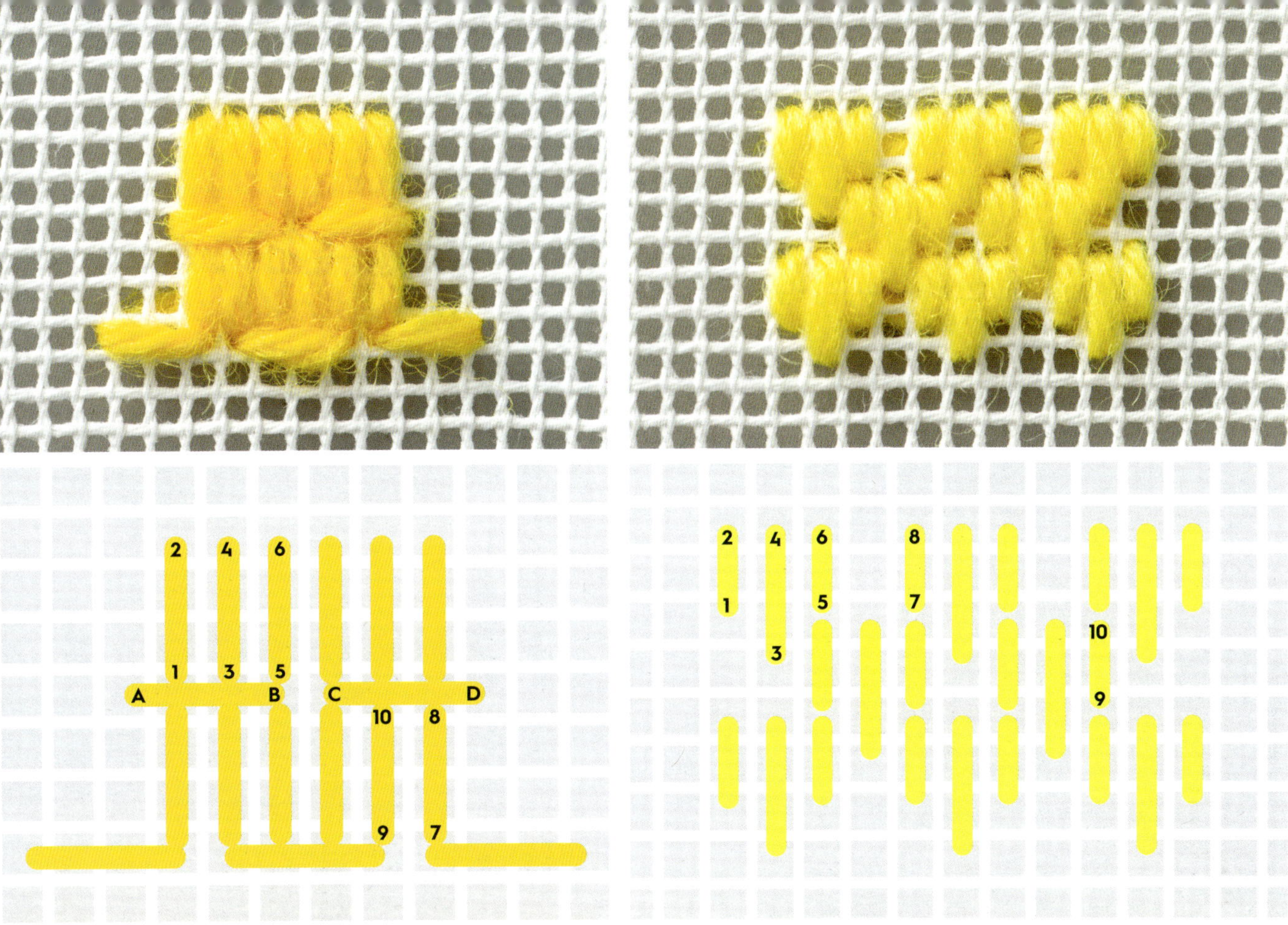

HALF DROPPED TIED STITCH

This stitch is very quick to work, with lots of easy straight stitches. Just make sure you pay attention to where you add your tied sections so the effect shows clearly.

- Working from left to right, bring the needle up at 1 and down through the canvas hole at 2, across three bars of canvas. Bring the needle up at 3 and down at 4, up at 5 and down at 6, and continue in this way until you have filled the desired area, working the next row from right to left directly below the one above.
- Now to stitch the ties. Bring the needle up at A and down at B, across three bars of canvas, then skip one bar and bring the needle up at C and down at D, again across three bars.

When working the ties on the next row, make sure they are off-centre from the row above.

HALF HUNGARIAN STITCH

This versatile little triangular stitch is great for small areas of canvas and incredibly easy to compensate.

- Working from left to right, bring the needle up at 1 and down through the canvas hole at 2, across two bars of canvas. Bring the needle up at 3 and down at 4, across three bars of canvas, then up at 5 and down at 6, across two bars of canvas. You have made your first half Hungarian stitch.
- Leaving a one canvas hole gap between each set of stitches and bringing the needle up at 7, work another three stitches as before.
- Continue in this way until you have a row filling the desired width.
- Working the next row in the opposite direction and bringing the needle up at 9, work each three-stitch set so that the longer stitches fit into the gaps left in the first row, as shown on the diagram.

Notice how all the smaller stitches line up one above the other.

For the Love of Flowers Notebook

Learn how to use long upright cross stitch to create stalks of lavender so realistic you can almost smell them. They feature alongside small brocade stitch roundels on an easy to construct notebook cover for the prettiest desk accessory. Refer to the making up section for the instructions and chart for this project.

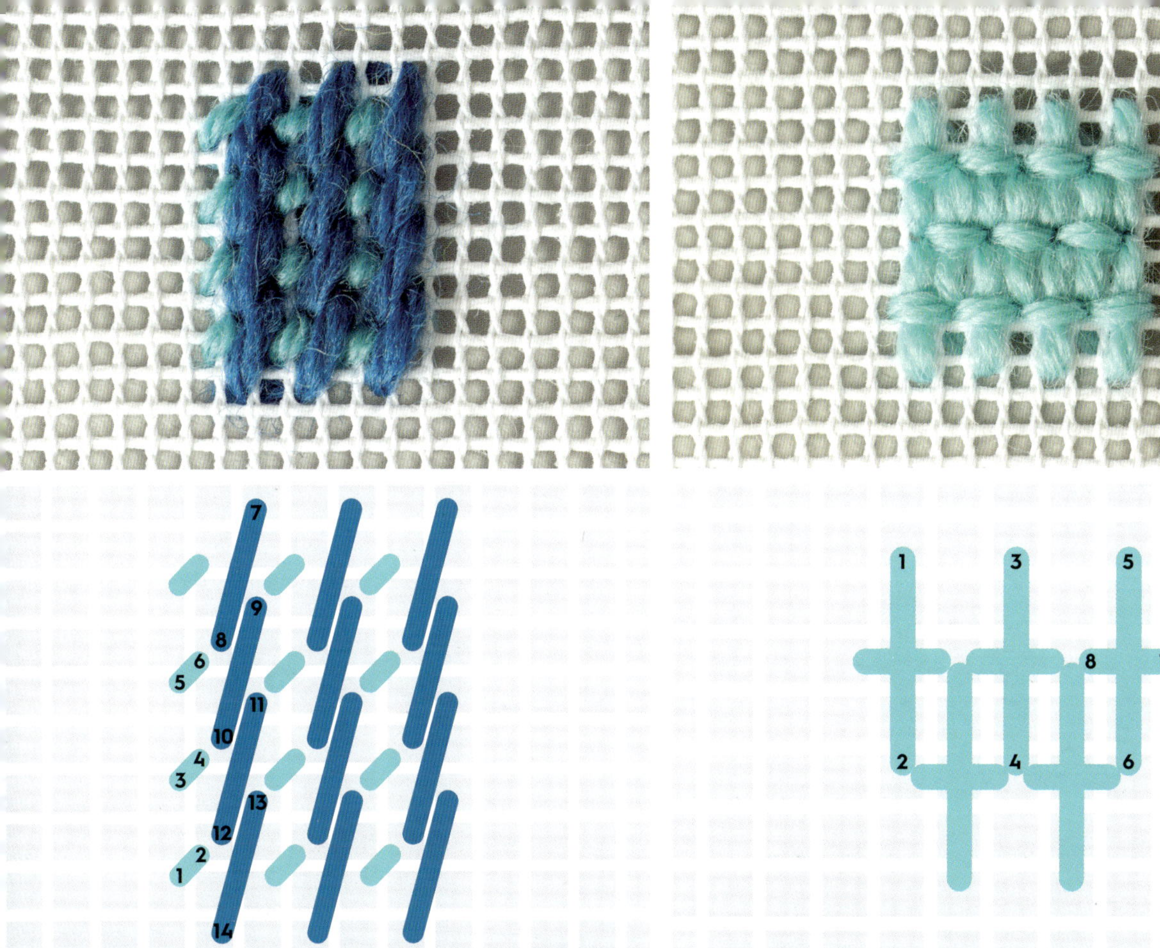

KENNAN STITCH

This stitch has most impact when worked in two colours, as shown in the stitched sample, particularly when using a lighter and darker shade.

- Working from bottom to top, bring the needle up at 1 and down through the canvas hole at 2, across one intersection of canvas, then skip a hole and bring the needle up at 3 and down at 4, again over one intersection of canvas. Continue in this way until you have a column filling the desired height.

For the second part of the stitch, the diagonal stitches become more elongated.

- Working from top to bottom, bring the needle up at 7 and down at 8, across three bars of canvas but stepping to the right across only one. Then skip one canvas hole to bring the needle up at 9 and down at 10.
- Continue to work these two columns until you have filled the desired width.

LONG UPRIGHT CROSS STITCH

You can use this stitch in small areas but I prefer it for medium sections, so you can get lots of the longer lengths in for greater impact.

- Working from left to right, bring the needle up at 1 and down through the canvas hole at 2, across four bars of canvas, then skip one canvas hole to bring the needle up at 3 and down at 4, again over four bars of canvas. Continue in this way until you have a row filling the desired width.
- Working in the opposite direction, complete the crosses by bringing the needle up at 7 and down at 8, across two bars of canvas, and continue to the end of the row.
- For the next row, stagger your stitches to fit into the gaps between the stitches in the row above, as shown in the diagram.

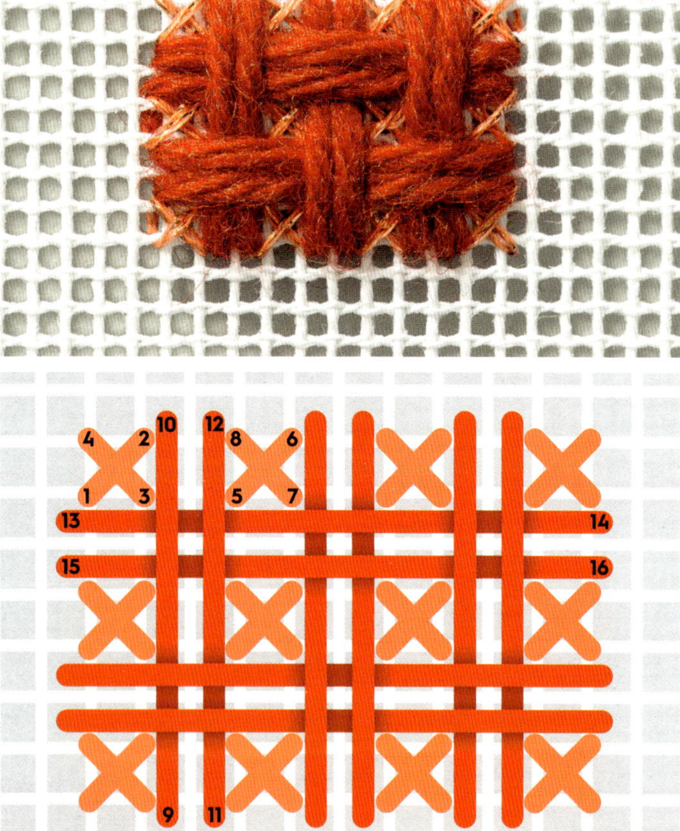

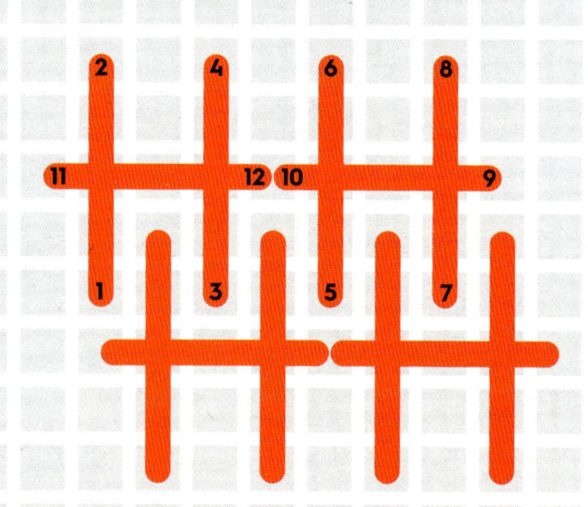

BUCKY'S WEAVING STITCH

The two-step process of this stitch, weaving lengths of thread between rows of cross stitch, creates a beautiful texture, shown here in two contrasting threads for extra pizazz.

- Working from left to right, bring the needle up at 1 and down at 2, across two intersections of canvas, then up at 3 and down at 4. Leaving one bar of canvas between stitches, bring the needle up at 5 and make another cross stitch, and continue in this way until you have a row filling the desired width. Work rows of cross stitch leaving one bar of canvas in between.

Now it's time to weave! Go as long as you dare! If you're stitching in a small-to-medium area, be brave; but on a larger area, set a length for each section to avoid baggy threads.

- Working from bottom to top, bring the needle up at 9 and down at 10, up at 11 and down at 12, and continue until you have a parallel pair of vertical threads between each column of cross stitches. This forms the warp for the weave.
- Working from left to right, bring the needle up at 13 and down at 14, up at 15 and down at 16, weaving under and over the warp threads and alternating the weave from row to row.

H STITCH

A big, bold textural stitch that gives you coverage really quickly. I love to use it to add texture to clothing on my designs, especially sweaters.

- Working from left to right, bring the needle up at 1 and down through the canvas hole at 2, across four bars of canvas. Then skip one canvas hole to bring the needle up at 3 and down at 4, again over four bars.
- Continue in this way until you have a row of vertical lengths filling the desired width.

Now working in the opposite direction, it's time to stitch the horizontal lengths across the row to form the H-shaped stitches.

- Bring the needle up at 9 and down at 10, across four bars of canvas, up at 11 and down at 12, and continue across the row.
- When starting the next row, make sure your stitches fit off-centre into the stitches in the row above, as shown in the diagram.

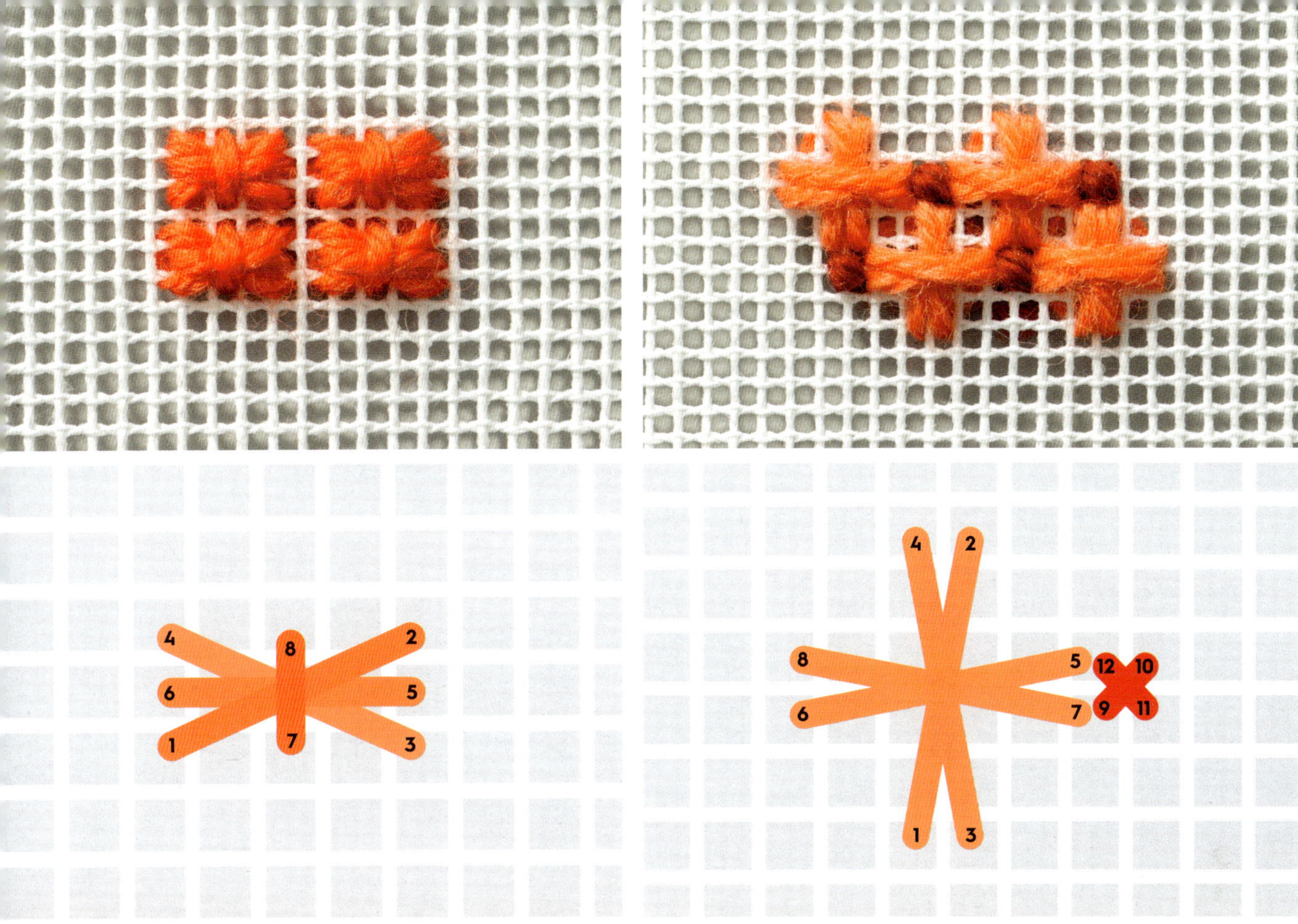

HORIZONTAL ELONGATED SMYRNA STITCH

This stitch reminds me of little bows or flags and it works particularly well in small areas.

- Bring the needle up at 1 and down through the canvas hole at 2, travelling at a slight diagonal that crosses four bars of canvas. Bring the needle up at 3 and down at 4.
- Bring the needle up at 5 and down at 6, across four bars of canvas, then up at 7 and down at 8, across two bars of canvas.
- To create a row of horizontal elongated Smyrna stitches, continue in this way leaving one bar of canvas between each stitch, as can be seen in the stitched sample.

LAYERED OBLIQUE CROSSES

This beautifully textured stitch is suited to medium-to-large areas as it needs to stretch out. It could easily make an eye-catching border, too.

- Bring the needle up at 1 and down through the canvas hole at 2, travelling at a slight diagonal that crosses five bars of canvas, then up at 3 and down at 4. Bring the needle up at 5 and down at 6, up at 7 and down at 8 to complete the large double cross.

Now stitch the tiny cross stitch to sit alongside the horizontal arm of your large double cross.

- Bring the needle up at 9 and down at 10, across one intersection, up at 11 and down at 12.
- To fill an area of your canvas, repeat these steps making sure you leave space at the end of the arms of each large cross for the smaller cross stitches to sit alongside.

CHOPSTICKS

This might look tricky to stitch when you first see it, but you'll soon get into the rhythm of stitching its alternating lengths.

- Working from top to bottom, bring the needle up at 1 and down through the canvas hole at 2, across two intersections of canvas but only travelling across one bar.
- Bring the needle up at 3 and down at 4 across one intersection of canvas, then up 5 and down at 6 for a diagonal stitch across one intersection in the opposite direction, to create a little V-shape.
- Continue in this way until you have a column filling the desired height.
- Working the next column from bottom to top, make sure the long diagonal stitches sit alongside the V-shaped stitches and vice versa (see stitches 7–12).

KNIT ONE, PURL ONE STITCH

This is the perfect stitch for textile details on canvas designs featuring clothing or soft furnishings. Just imagine it on a tiny sweater!

- Working from bottom to top, bring the needle up at 1 and down through the canvas hole at 2, across one bar of canvas, then up at 3 and down at 4, again across one bar. Continue in this way until you have a column filling the desired height.
- Working the next column in the opposite direction, bring the needle up at 7 and down at 8 across one intersection of canvas, then up at 9 and down at 10, for a diagonal stitch across one intersection in the opposite direction, to create a little V-shaped stitch, and continue in this way to the bottom of the column.
- Working from bottom to top, repeat the working of the horizontal straight stitches from the first column, as shown in the diagram.

RISE AND SHINE MIRROR FRAME

THE BEAUTIFULLY TEXTURED KENNAN STITCH HAS BEEN USED TO WORK THE SUN JUST BEGINNING TO RISE BEHIND THE CLOUDS. REFER TO THE MAKING UP SECTION FOR THE INSTRUCTIONS AND CHART FOR THIS PROJECT.

SKY

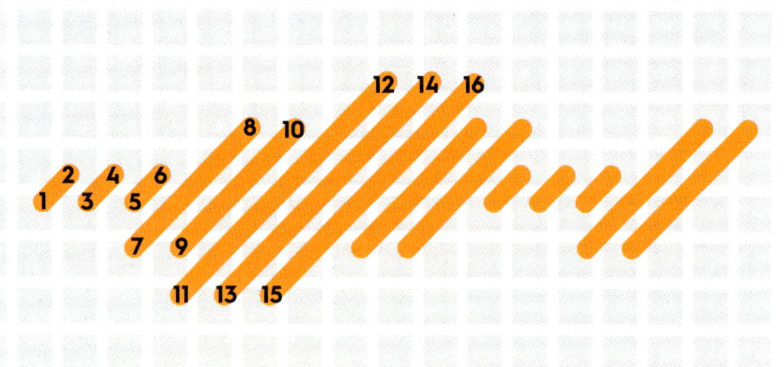

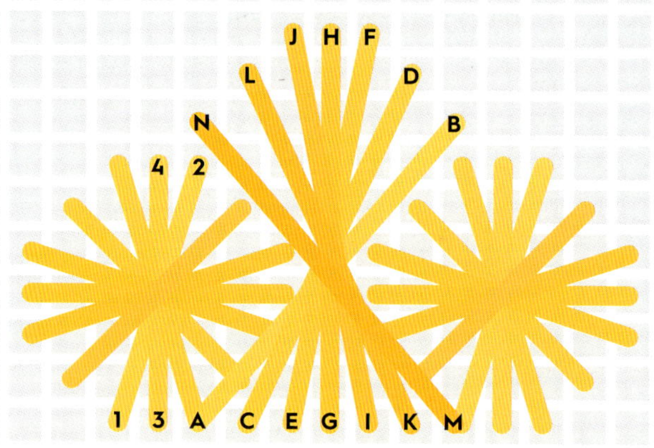

SWIRL STITCH

This stitch has a cloud-like shape that lends itself perfectly to texturing a sky background or detailing a cloud.

+ Working from left to right, bring the needle up at 1 and down through the canvas hole at 2, across one intersection of canvas, then up at 3 and down at 4, up at 5 and down at 6.
+ Stepping down one canvas hole beneath the starting point of the previous stitch, bring the needle up at 7 and down at 8, across three intersections, then up at 9 and down at 10.
+ Again, stepping down one canvas hole beneath the starting point of the previous stitch, bring the needle up at 11 and down at 12, across five intersections of canvas, then up at 13 and down at 14, up at 15 and down at 16.
+ Following the diagram carefully for the starting points, begin to decrease the length of your diagonal stitches, making two more over three intersections of canvas, and three more over one intersection, and continue until you have a row filling the desired width.

On the next row, the shortest stitches should sit beneath the longest stitches above.

RHODES CLOUD

Place a Rhodes octagon either side of a half Rhodes stitch and you get a Rhodes cloud – a stitch I invented to capture the soft puffy quality of cumulus clouds.

+ Bring the needle up at 1 and down through the canvas hole at 2, across six bars of canvas. Then up at 3 and down at 4, and continue in this way, working anticlockwise to form the octagon shape.

Carefully count how many bars each stitch covers to ensure you achieve the correct shape.

+ Leaving five empty canvas holes from the base of the first Rhodes octagon, stitch another exactly the same.

There should be one canvas hole between the Rhodes octagons at their closest point. Now for the fun bit!

+ Bring the needle up at A and down through the canvas hole at B, bring the needle up at C and down at D, and continue to follow the marked letter sequence to create a fan-shape, completing the Rhodes cloud.

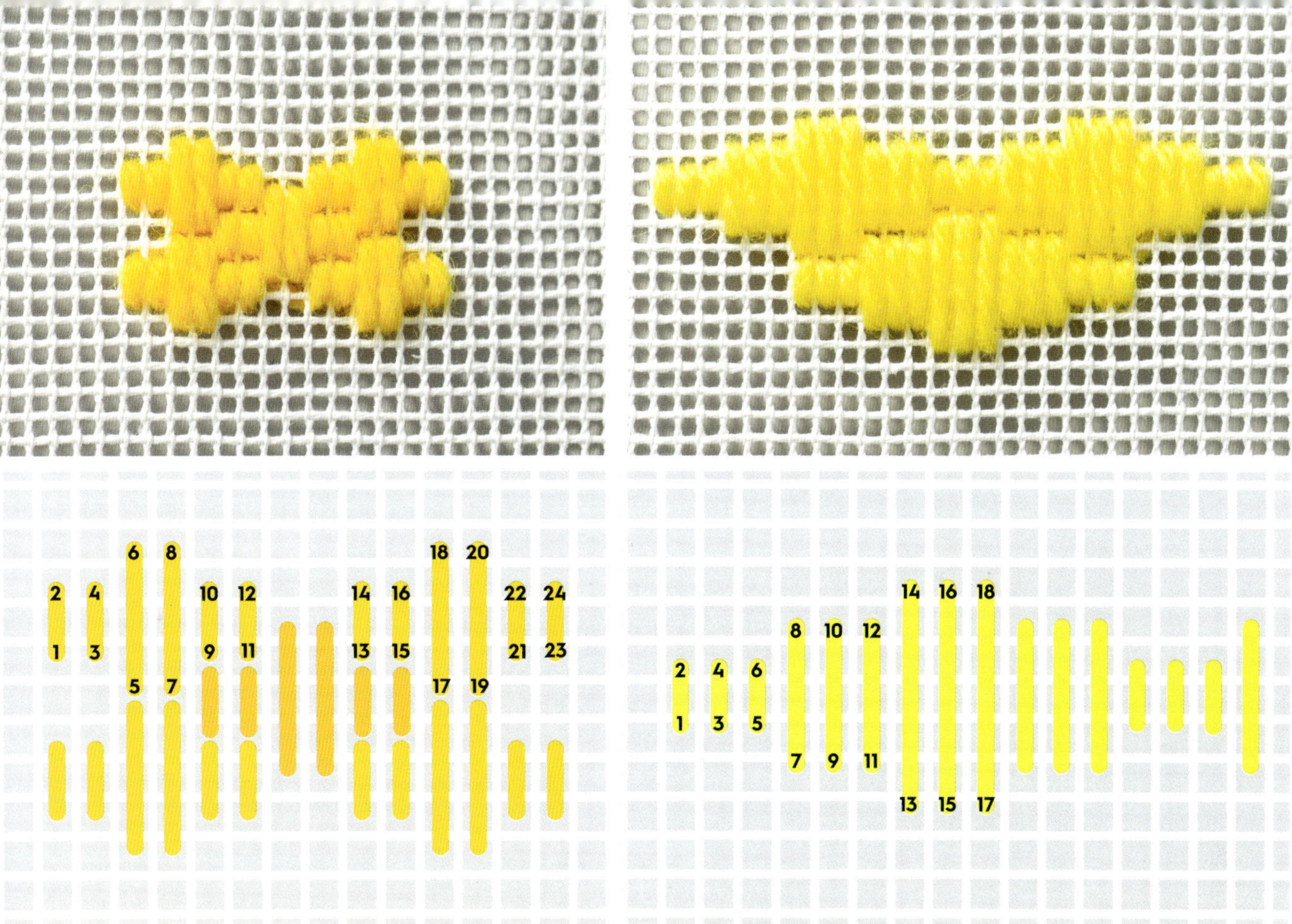

DOUBLE HUNGARIAN STITCH

This is another of my favourites to create cloud shapes. It's beautiful all worked in one colour, but try mixing in a white every now and then to accentuate the shape.

- Working from left to right, bring the needle up at 1 and down through the canvas hole at 2, across two bars of canvas, then up at 3 and down at 4.
- Bring the needle up at 5 and down at 6, across four bars of canvas, then up at 7 and down at 8.
- Bring the needle up at 9 and down at 10, across two bars of canvas, then up at 11 and down at 12 to complete the stitch.
- Leaving a gap of two canvas holes, start your next double Hungarian stitch (13 to 24), and continue in this way until you have a row filling the desired width.
- Working the next and subsequent rows, make sure the shorter stitches all sit perfectly under each other, with the longer stitches stretching up into the gap in between, as seen in the stitched sample.

TRIPLE HUNGARIAN STITCH

Really just an extended version of double Hungarian stitch, this creates a softer look as it graduates gently up and down – fabulous for a pillowy cloud vibe!

- Working from left to right, bring the needle up at 1 and down through the canvas hole at 2, across two bars of canvas, then up at 3 and down at 4, up at 5 and down at 6, again over two bars each time.
- Bring the needle up at 7 and down at 8, this time across four bars of canvas, up at 9 and down at 10, up at 11 and down at 12.
- Bring the needle up at 13 and down at 14, this time across six bars of canvas, up at 15 and down at 16, up at 17 and down at 18.
- Now start to decrease your stitch lengths again, repeating the triple sets of four-bar and two-bar stitches as shown on the diagram, and continue in this way until you have a row filling the desired width.
- Working the next and subsequent rows, make sure the sets of short two-bar and long six-bar stitches are perfectly aligned with each other, as shown in the stitched sample.

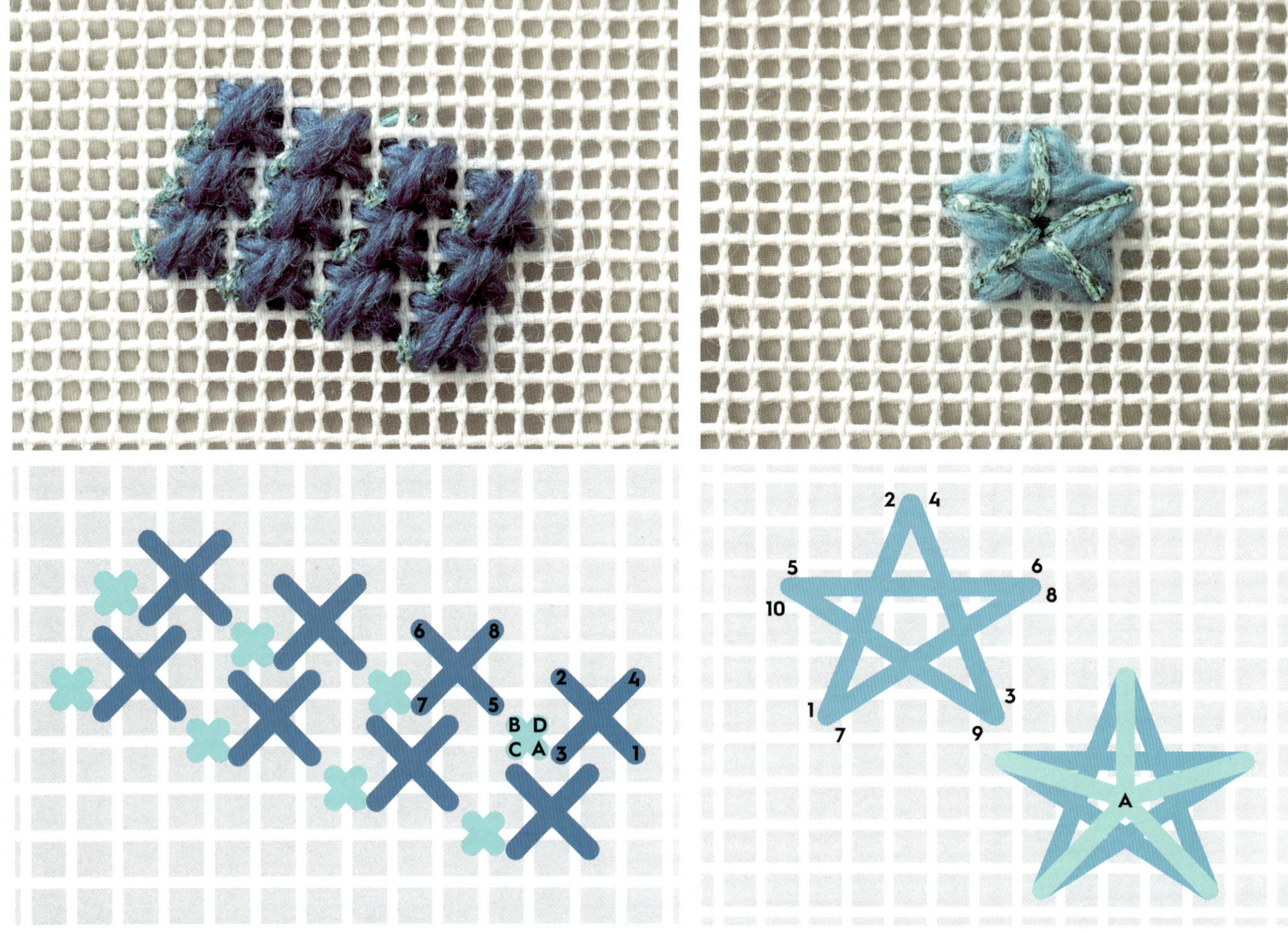

STAGGERED CROSS STITCH

Do you have a canvas that needs a starry night sky? This could be the stitch for you! I've added a metallic thread in the mix to really give it some sparkle.

I find the best way to approach this stitch is one row at a time, alternating the working of the large and small cross stitch rows.

- Working from right to left, bring the needle up at 1 and down through the canvas hole at 2, across two intersections of canvas. Then bring the needle up at 3 and down at 4, to make your first large cross stitch.
- To create the next large cross stitch, bring the needle up at 5 (in the hole below 2, one bar to the left), down at 6, up at 7 and down at 8. Continue staggering the cross stitches in this way to reach the height of your canvas area.
- Again working from right to left, now work a row of small cross stitches at the base of each large cross stitch. Bring the needle up at A and down through the canvas hole at B, across one intersection. Then up at C and down at D, and continue across your canvas, as seen in the diagram.

EYELET STARS

If you are looking for a stitch to create a highlight in your night sky, this might just be it. Stitched in two stages, it's really two stitches in one!

The first stage is to stitch the five-point background star.

- Bring the needle up at 1 and down through the canvas hole at 2, to make a diagonal stitch across five bars of canvas, then up at 3 and down at 4. Bring the needle up at 5 and down at 6, again across five bars of canvas, to make a horizontal stitch. Then continuing with diagonal stitches, bring the needle up at 7 and down at 8, up at 9 and down at 10, to complete the star.

The second stage is to work the eyelet on top of the background star, and this is best worked in a thinner thread.

- Bring the needle up at one of the points of the background star and take it down into the canvas hole at the centre of the star, marked A on the diagram. Bring the needle up at the next point and down into the centre once again, and continue in this way to complete the eyelet star.

STAR DASH CROSS STITCH

With its two different sizes of star – a simple small cross and a large eight-pointed star – this works well to fill in large background areas.

This stitch lends itself to using a metallic thread to highlight parts of the design, as I did for the dashes.

+ Working from left to right, bring the needle up at 1 and down through the canvas hole at 2, across two bars of canvas, then up at 3 and down at 4 to complete the small cross star stitch.
+ Skip one bar of canvas to bring the needle up at 5 and down at 6, across two bars of canvas, to create the dash stitch.
+ Continue to stitch these two stitches in this way, to create a grid to fill the width and height of your desired area.

Now to fill in the gaps in the grid with the large eight-pointed stars.

+ Bring the needle up at A and down at B, across four bars of canvas, and up at C and down at D. Then bring the needle up at E and down at F, across two intersections, and up at G and down at H.

SIRNA STAR STITCH

These starburst stitches are for those looking for something a bit jazzier for their skies.

+ Working from left to right, bring the needle up at 1 and down through the canvas hole at 2, across seven bars of canvas at a slight diagonal.
+ Stepping up one hole diagonally each time, bring the needle up at 3 and down at 4, up at 5 and down at 6, up at 7 and down at 8, up at 9 and down at 10, carefully following the diagram to complete the first Sirna star in the row.
+ To work the next Sirna star, line up your starting point with stitch 5 to 6 (the middle stitch of the previous star), and bring your needle up at 11 and down at 12, and continue in this way until you have a row filling the desired width.
+ To line your stitches up perfectly on the next row, just remember that your starting point is six holes beneath point 3 in the star above.

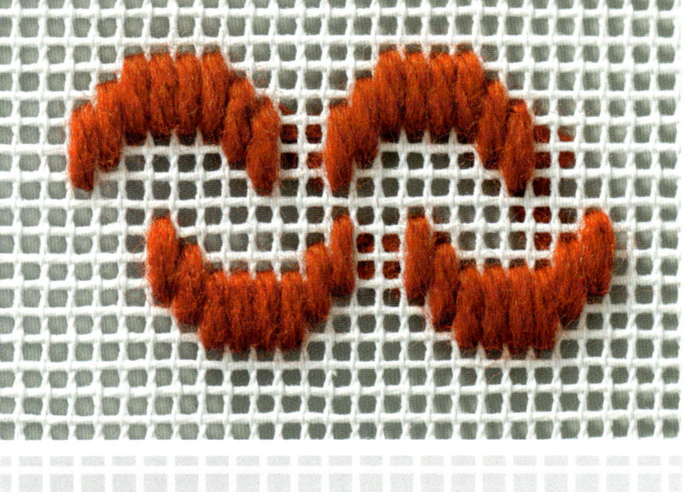

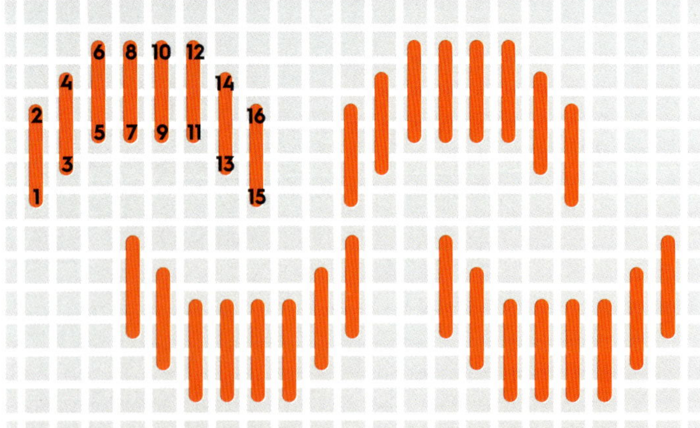

CRESCENT STITCH

This little stitch is so easy to learn and works brilliantly on backgrounds. You can work it individually, too – turn 90 degrees to the right to make a waxing moon, or 90 degrees to the left for a waning moon!

- Working from left to right, bring the needle up at 1 and down through the canvas hole at 2, across three bars of canvas.
- Taking a step up, bring the needle up at 3 and down at 4, again across three bars of canvas.
- Take another step up, bring the needle up at 5 and down at 6, across three bars of canvas, then make three more parallel stitches (7 to 8, 9 to 10, 11 to 12), before stepping your stitches back down to complete the crescent shape, as shown in the diagram. Leave two empty canvas holes between crescents when working them in a row.

To start a new row, just do the same again, or mirror and stagger them as I have done in the stitched sample.

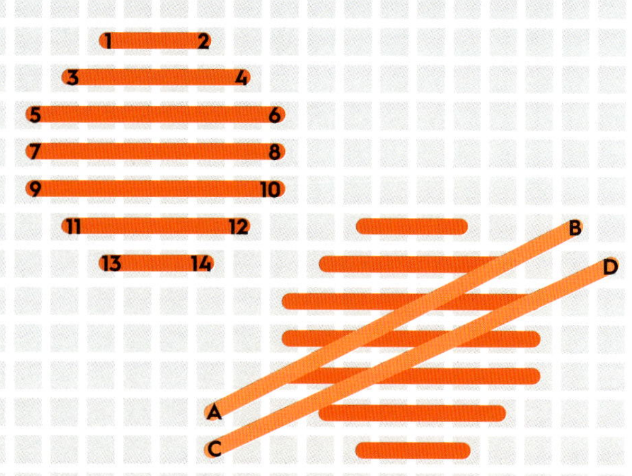

SATURN STITCH

This is a stitch I invented after a dear friend misheard me say 'satin stitch'! I just knew it would make the perfect addition to a celestial canvas.

- Bring the needle up at 1 and down through the canvas hole at 2, across three bars of canvas, then up at 3 and down at 4, across five bars of canvas. Bring the needle up at 5 and down at 6, across seven bars of canvas and repeat to make two more parallel stitches (7 to 8, 9 to 10).
- Now bring the needle up at 11 and down at 12, up at 13 and down at 14, to mirror the top half of the planet.
- To create Saturn's rings, bring the needle up at A and down at B, up at C and down at D. (Note how stitch C to D is slightly longer than stitch A to B.)

Randomly dot your Saturn stitches around your canvas for best effect.

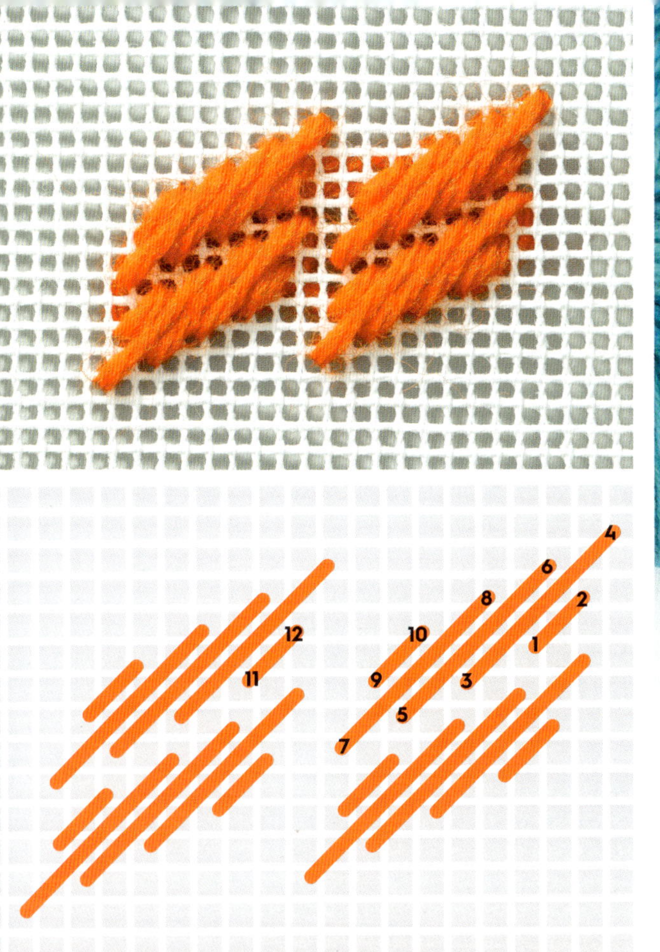

LIGHTNING BOLT

The perfect stitch if you are searching for some drama in your skyscape! It always looks great whether worked together, as shown here, or stitched in isolation and randomly scattered about your canvas.

- Working from right to left, bring the needle up at 1 and down through the canvas hole at 2, across two intersections of canvas. Bring the needle up at 3 and down at 4, up at 7 and down at 8, working each of these stitches across five intersections of canvas. Then up at 9 and down at 10, over two intersections to complete your first lightning bolt.
- To start your next lightning bolt, count four canvas holes to the left from 9, to bring the needle up at 11 and down at 12, and continue as before.

VARIEGATED THREADS

ONE SUREFIRE WAY OF ADDING A BIT OF INTEREST TO LARGE AREAS OF CANVAS IS TO WORK THEM IN VARIEGATED THREADS, WHICH ARE THREADS DYED IN VARYING COLOURS OR IN TONAL SHADES OF ONE COLOUR. I'VE RECENTLY DISCOVERED THE JOYS OF STITCHING WITH VARIEGATED THREADS THANKS TO MY FRIEND KITEY, AKA THE YARN WHISPERER, AN AMAZING HAND DYER WHO HAS JUST BRANCHED OUT INTO TAPESTRY WOOLS.

STITCHING WITH VARIEGATED THREADS IS A BIT LIKE PAINTING, AS THE COLOURS HAVE AN ELEMENT OF THE RANDOM ABOUT THEM. AS YOU WORK ACROSS THE CANVAS, POPS OF LIGHT AND DARK COLOUR ADD A TOTALLY DIFFERENT DIMENSION AND A SENSE OF REALISM... AND BOY DO THEY WORK WELL FOR SKIES!

AS MUCH AS WE ALL LOVE A GOOD NEEDLEPOINT STITCHING SESSION, WHEN FACED WITH A HUGE EXPANSE OF ONE COLOUR IT CAN SOMETIMES FEEL A BIT OF A CHORE. BUT IF YOU CHOOSE TO WORK THESE AREAS IN VARIEGATED THREADS IT'LL FEEL A GOOD DEAL LESS HUMDRUM, AND YOUR PROJECT WILL BE TRANSFORMED BY THE EXPERIENCE TOO!

ELEMENTAL COASTERS

THIS PROJECT BRINGS TOGETHER STITCHES FROM THE SCENIC STITCH COLLECTIONS IN THIS BOOK, FROM THE SKY, LAND AND WATER CHAPTERS, TO EXPLORE THE FOUR ELEMENTS IN VARIEGATED THREADS. REFER TO THE MAKING UP SECTION FOR THE INSTRUCTIONS AND CHART FOR THIS PROJECT.

SKIP TENT POLKA

A perfect snow stitch for winter skies! It would look really lovely worked in a textured thread, or include an odd metallic thread stitch here and there.

- Working from bottom to top, bring the needle up at 1 and down through the canvas hole at 2, across one intersection of canvas, then skipping a hole bring the needle up at 3 and down at 4. Continue in this way until you have a column filling the desired height.
- Working the next column from top to bottom and leaving one bar of canvas in between, bring the needle up at 5 and down at 6 across one intersection, up at 7 and down at 8.
- Continue in this way to fill the desired area, lining up the stitches diagonally across the gap between columns.

SKIP T STITCH

This beautiful open stitch perfectly captures the effect of snow falling through the sky, but it could even work for a starry sky!

- Working from bottom to top, bring the needle up at 1 and down through the canvas hole at 2, across one intersection. Skipping one canvas hole above, bring the needle up at 3 and down at 4. Continue in this way until you have a column filling the desired height.

The angle of the working of the stitches is alternated in each column, leaving one bar of canvas empty in between columns.

- Working from top to bottom, bring the needle up at 5 and down at 6, up at 7 and down at 8, and continue in this way.

WATER

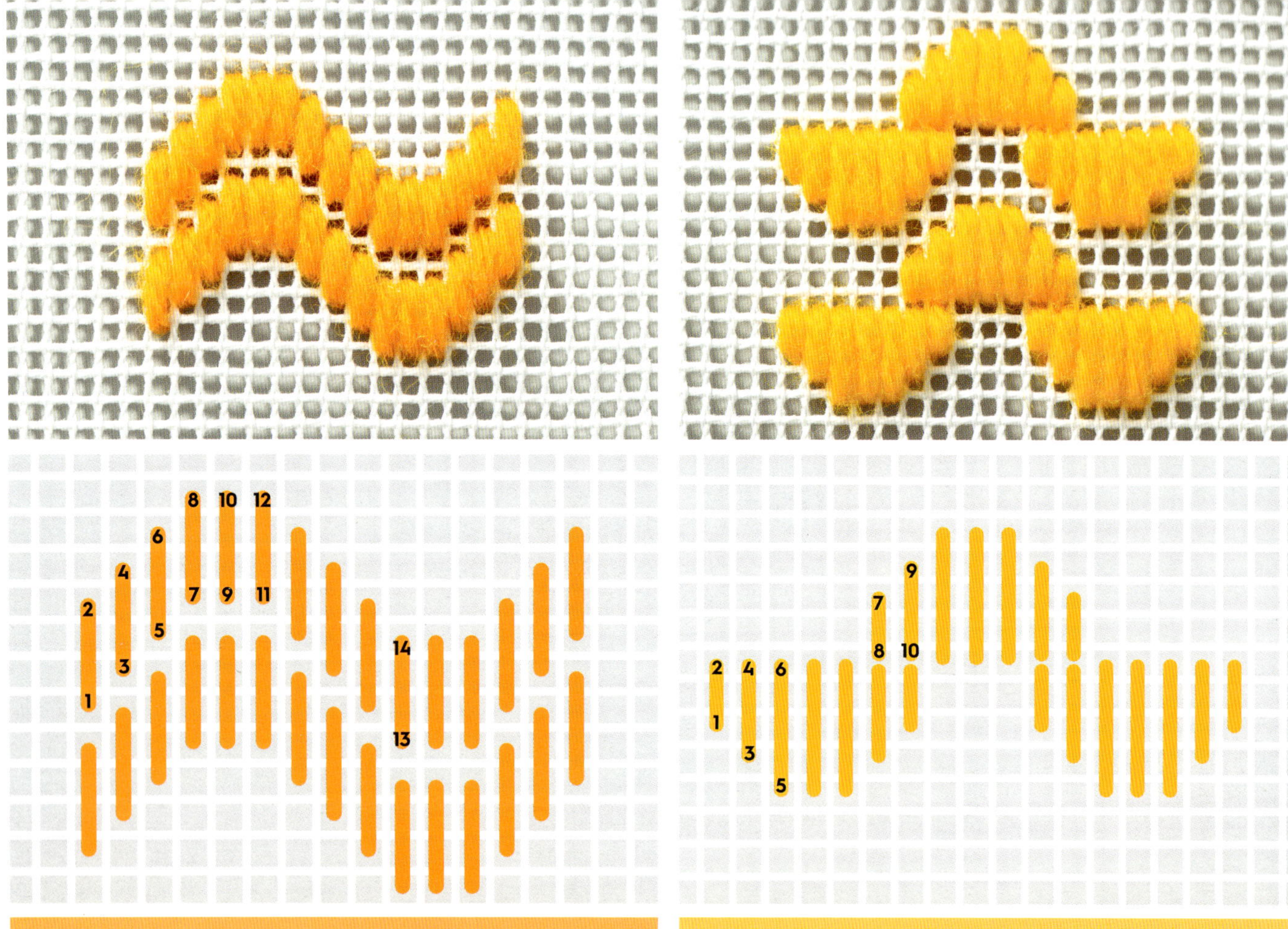

OPEN WAVE STITCH

This stitch can be worked with all the rows joining, but I much prefer it as shown here with a bar's gap in between to really accentuate the flowing shapes.

- Working from left to right, bring the needle up at 1 and down through the canvas hole at 2, across three bars of canvas.
- Taking a step up each time, bring the needle up at 3 and down at 4, up at 5 and down at 6, up at 7 and down at 8, again across three bars of canvas. Then make two parallel stitches to create the crest of your wave, before stepping your stitches back down to mirror the rise of your wave, until you reach 13 to 14, as shown in the diagram.
- Continue in this way to create the rise and fall of the waves until you have a row filling the desired width

SCALLOP ROW STITCH

This open stitch works best on large areas of canvas. As it shows a lot of the canvas underneath, you can really have a lot of fun playing with contrasting tones.

- Working from left to right, bring the needle up at 1 and down through the canvas hole at 2, across two bars of canvas, then up at 3 and down at 4, across three bars.
- Bring the needle up at 5 and down at 6, across four bars, then stitch two more parallel stitches before decreasing again to complete your first scallop.
- To make the next scallop in the row, bring the needle up at 7 and down at 8, across two bars of canvas, to align with the decreasing three-bar stitch of the scallop below, and continue to stitch scallops in this way, as shown in the diagram, until you have a row filling the desired width.
- The starting point for the first stitch in the next row will be seven holes beneath the starting point of the first stitch of the scallop in the row above, for a two-hole gap between rows.

INVERTED SCALLOPS

This instantly brings mermaids to mind; a perfect pattern for larger projects.

+ Working from left to right, bring the needle up at 1 and down at 2, across three bars of canvas. Bring the needle up at 3 and down at 4, up at 5 and down at 6 to complete a set of three parallel stitches.
+ Stepping up by one hole each time, bring the needle up at 7 and down at 8, across three bars, then up at 9 and down at 10, across four bars. Stepping up by two holes this time, bring the needle up at 11 and down at 12, across four bars. Now mirror the shape to work your way down again.
+ Continue in this way until you have a row of scallop edging filling the desired width. Note stitch 21 to 22 is both the last stitch of one scallop and the first stitch of the next.

Stagger rows of scallop edging, then fill the section in between rows, as follows:

+ Bring the needle up at 23 and down at 24, across two bars, up at 25 and down at 26, across four bars, up at 27 and down at 28, across six bars, up at 29 and down at 30, across seven bars and up at 31 and down at 32, across nine bars, and decreasing back down again (33 to 40).

METALLIC THREADS

METALLIC THREADS HAVE A BIT OF A BAD NAME AMONGST THE STITCHING COMMUNITY, AS MANY CAN BE REALLY TRICKY TO WORK WITH. INDEED, STITCHERS HAVE BEEN KNOWN TO THROW THEIR PROJECTS ACROSS THE ROOM OUT OF SHEER METALLIC-THREAD FRUSTRATION! BUT WHY DENY YOURSELF THE FUN OF ADDING A BIT OF GLITZ AND LIGHT-CATCHING SPARKLE TO YOUR PROJECTS WHEN I CAN STEER YOU RIGHT?

KREINIK'S METALLIC THREADS ARE MY PERSONAL FAVOURITES. THEY OFFER A GREAT RANGE OF COLOURS AND BRAID THICKNESSES, AND THERE'S SOMETHING ABOUT HOW THEY ARE SPUN THAT MAKES THEM SO LOVELY TO STITCH WITH, SO THEY DON'T FIGHT WITH THE CANVAS LIKE SOME METALLIC THREADS DO. I'VE USED THEM TO STITCH FISH SCALES, GEMS, SUNRAYS, AND SO MUCH MORE, AND, HONESTLY, THEIR JEWEL-LIKE TONES ARE AN ABSOLUTE DELIGHT.

ANOTHER STRONG CONTENDER IS RAINBOW GALLERY, WHO HAVE A HUGE COLLECTION OF DIFFERENT TYPES OF METALLICS, WITH PLENTY THAT ARE BLENDED WITH OTHER FIBRES, WHICH MAKES THEM A LOT SOFTER TO WORK WITH.

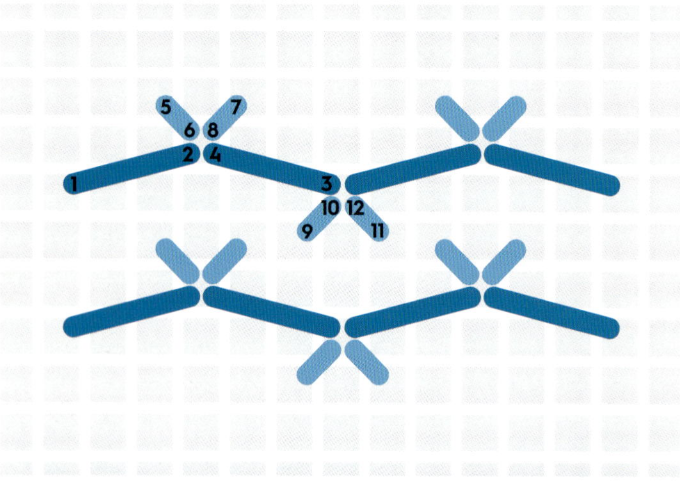

ALTERNATING TINY CROWNS

This open stitch is the ideal candidate for capturing rough seas for stormier seascapes.

- Working from left to right, bring the needle up at 1 and down through the canvas hole at 2, across three bars of canvas at a slight diagonal. Then up at 3 and down at 4 to mirror your first stitch.

Now to top and tail your elongated diagonal stitches.

- Bring the needle up at 5 and down at 6 across one intersection, then up at 7 and down at 8, noticing how these short stitches share the same canvas hole as the longer stitches. Then on the underside of the row, bring the needle up at 9 and down at 10, up at 11 and down at 12.
- Continue in this way until you have a row filling the desired width.
- The starting point for the first stitch in the next row will be three holes beneath the first stitch of the row above, ensuring a one-hole gap between the rows as shown on the diagram.

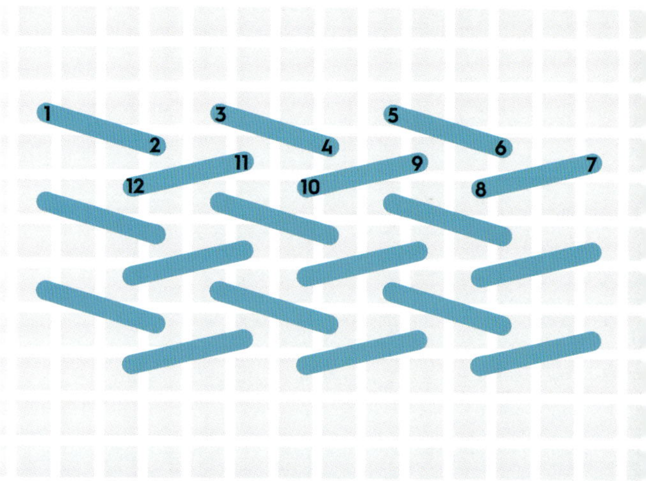

OPEN WATER STITCH

This dynamic zigzagging stitch is brilliant if you are looking for a choppy water effect.

- Working from left to right, bring the needle up at 1 and down through the canvas hole at 2, across three bars of canvas at a slight diagonal. Bring the needle up at 3 and down at 4, up at 5 and down at 6, and continue until you have reached the width of your canvas.

Note how the starting point of each stitch is four canvas holes away from the last.

- To create your next row, working from right to left, bring the needle up at 7 and down at 8, up at 9 and down at 10, up at 11 and down at 12, working your stitches in the opposite direction to those on the row above.

DAVID'S WATER STITCH

This takes the open water stitch and gives it a little extra detail that I've found is best worked in a metallic thread, to give the impression of sunlight reflecting on choppy seas.

+ First work the rows of long diagonal stitches, following the instructions for the open water stitch. This time I have started my first row by working from right to left.

Once you have filled the desired area, it's time to add the small stitch details in between the diagonal stitches.

+ Work small diagonal stitches across a single intersection of canvas in the spaces before and in between the longer diagonal stitches on each row, but in the opposite direction to them (1 to 2, 3 to 4, 5 to 6). Remember to change direction on the next row (7 to 8, 9 to 10).

SHORT FLAGS HORIZONTAL

Often used for roof tiles and brickwork, this might not seem an obvious choice, but trust me, with the right thread this makes a fabulous water stitch. Work it in blue tones, or metallics, and you'll be transported to the coast.

+ Working from right to left, bring the needle up at 1 and down through the canvas hole at 2, across one intersection of canvas, up at 3 and down at 4, again across one intersection.
+ Bring the needle up at 5 and down at 6, across three intersections of canvas, then stitch two more parallel stitches (7 to 8, 9 to 10), to create your first flag.
+ To start the next flag, bring the needle up at 11 and down at 12, so your first stitch lines up perfectly with the last stitch in the flag before.
+ Continue in this way across the canvas and to add another diagonal row of flags, leave at least one bar of canvas in between as shown in the diagram.

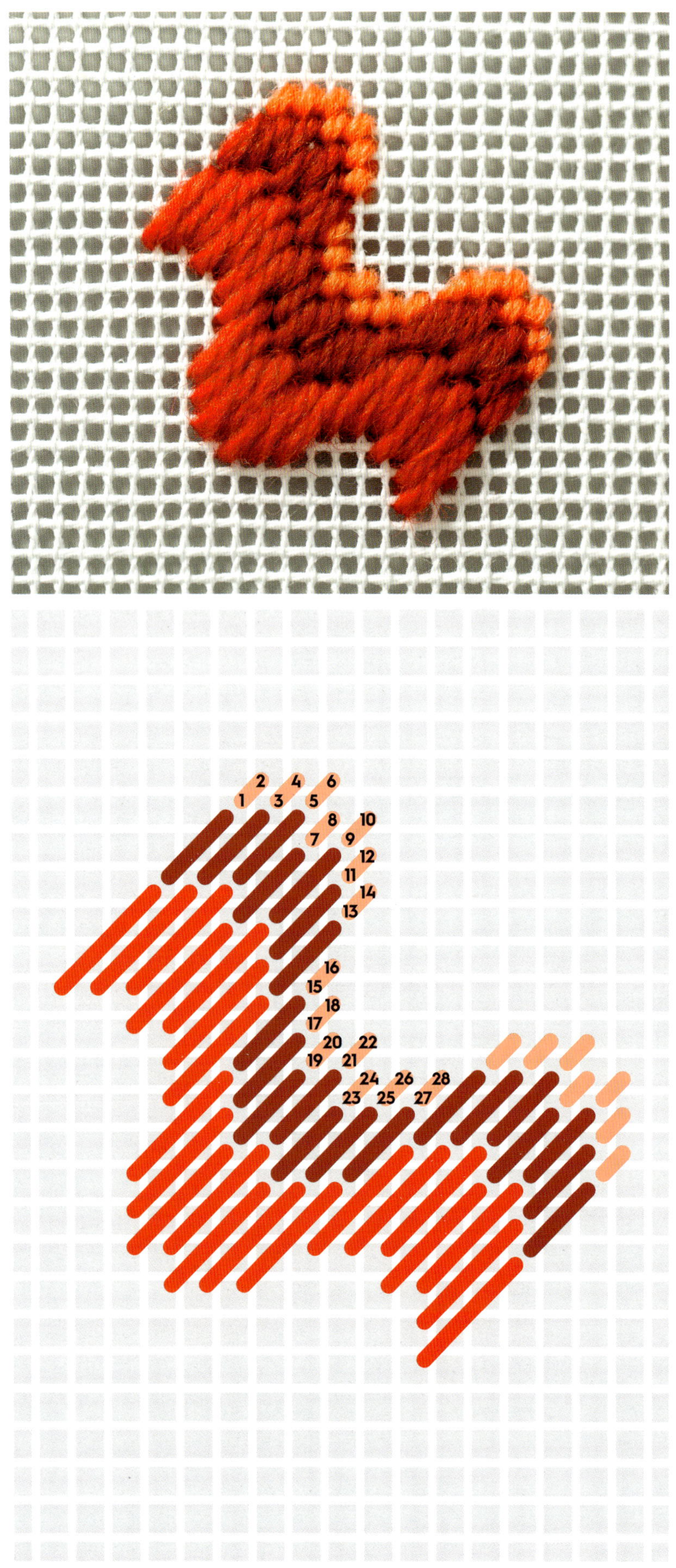

BARGELLO WAVE STITCH

At first glance this stitch can look a bit tricky, but as it's worked on perfect diagonals it's actually incredibly easy. Once you have your first row of stitches, you'll be flying through it.

+ The first row is worked in tent stitch and establishes the flow of the pattern. Working from top to bottom, bring the needle up at 1 and down through the canvas hole at 2, across one intersection of canvas. Create two more parallel stitches, 3 to 4, 5 to 6. Then step down a canvas hole to work 7 to 8, and 9 to 10. Step down a canvas hole for 11 to 12, and step down again for 13 to 14.
+ Now, bring the needle up at 15 and down at 16, and continue to follow the stitching path as shown on the diagram. You are basically working the first run of stitches (1 to 14) to reverse the shape, finishing by bringing the needle up at 27 and down at 28. Notice that there is a one bar gap in between the top (curve) and the bottom (dip) line of stitches. Continue to alternate these curve and dip sections of tent stitch until you have reached the desired height and width of your canvas.
+ For the second row, line up your stitches with your first row of stitches, working across two intersections of canvas. For the third row, line up your stitches with your second row of stitches, this time working across three intersections of canvas. Continue across your canvas repeating these three rows.

If you're in the mood to experiment, try varying the order of the rows. It can look impressive worked 1- 2 - 3 - 2 - 1, for example.

BESIDE THE SEA BEACH BAG

NOTICE HERE HOW USING DIFFERENT TONES AND COLOURS CAN GIVE DEPTH TO A DESIGN WHILST WORKING THE SEA WITH BARGELLO WAVE STITCH. REFER TO THE MAKING UP SECTION FOR THE INSTRUCTIONS AND CHART FOR THIS PROJECT.

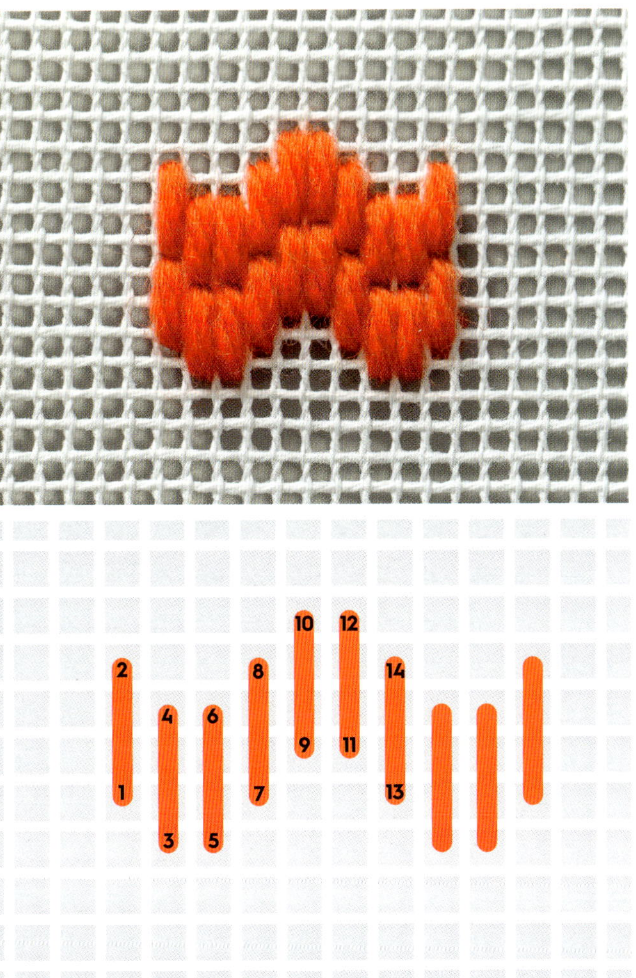

MINI WAVE STITCH

This stitch is perfect when you want a water wave but only have a small section to fill.

- Working from left to right, bring the needle up at 1 and down through the canvas hole at 2, across three bars of canvas. Stepping down one canvas hole, bring the needle up at 3 and down at 4, then up at 5 and down at 6. Stepping up one canvas hole this time, bring the needle up at 7 and down at 8, then up 9 and down at 10. Then bring the needle up at 11 and down at 12 to complete the top of your wave.
- Continue in this way until you have a row filling the desired width, and work subsequent rows to line up perfectly with the one above, as seen in the stitched sample.

MEDIEVAL MOSAIC STITCH

This produces a subtle ripple worked in a single colour; for a more dramatic effect, work it in multiple shades.

+ Working from top to bottom, bring the needle up at 1 and down through the canvas hole at 2, up at 3 and down at 4, up at 5 and down at 6, up at 7 and down at 8. Each stitch is worked across four bars of canvas, stepping one hole to the side each time.
+ Now bring the needle up at 9 and down at 10 across two bars of canvas, so that this shorter stitch lines up with the middle section of the longer stitch above it. Bring the needle up at 11 and down at 12, up at 13 and down at 14, up at 15 and down at 16, working each stitch across two bars of canvas, stepping one hole to the side each time.
+ Bring the needle up at 17 and down at 18 and continue to stitch long and short sets of stitches in this way until you have a column filling the desired height.
+ Working the next column, make sure the long stitches are next to the short stitches and vice versa, as shown in the stitched sample.

OBLIQUE PAIRS

Such a simple, sweet and easy stitch that quickly builds up to give you an effective wave for any canvas.

+ Working from left to right, bring the needle up at 1 and down through the canvas hole at 2, across four bars of canvas at a slight diagonal. Bring the needle up at 3 and down at 4 to create a parallel stitch, completing your first pair of stitches.
+ Bring the needle up at 5 and down at 6, and up at 7 and down at 8, and continue to create pairs of stitches in this way until you have a row filling the desired width.
+ Working the next row from right to left, leave one empty hole from the row above to bring your needle up at 9 and down at 10, and continue as before, lining your pairs of stitches up along the row.

BARGELLO CREST

You'll need a large area of canvas to show this off properly. This can look complicated to do, but like all things stitch, just establish a starting line and the rest falls into place.

- Working from left to right, bring the needle up at 1 and down through the canvas hole at 2, across three intersections of canvas. Stepping up one canvas hole each time, bring the needle up at 3 and down at 4, repeating eight times to make a total of nine stitches ending with the stitch marked 5 to 6.
- Then bring the needle up at 7 and down at 8, alongside the stitch marked 5 to 6, and make another three parallel diagonal stitches, as shown in the diagram.
- Now stepping down one canvas hole, make two parallel diagonal stitches, 9 and 10 and 11 and 12. Repeat to make two more identical pairs of stitches.
- Stepping down one canvas hole, bring the needle up at 13 and down at 14, and up at 15 and down at 16 to complete the Bargello crest.
- Stitch 15 to 16 becomes stitch 1 to 2 of the next Bargello crest in the row as you continue to repeat this pattern across the row.

Note that all the stitches are worked across three intersections of the canvas.

RIPPLE STITCH

When we're choosing stitches to depict water, horizontal stitches may be the obvious choice, but this vertically worked stitch will make you think again.

- Working from top to bottom, bring the needle up at 1 and down through the canvas hole at 2, across five bars of canvas. Skipping one bar of canvas, bring the needle up at 3 and down at 4, across five bars of canvas, up at 5 and down at 6, across four bars, up at 7 and down at 8, also across four bars, then up at 9 and down at 10, across five bars.
- Leaving one bar of canvas in between, bring the needle up at 11 and down at 12 and mirror the stitches numbered 3–10.
- Working from bottom to top for the next column, leaving two empty canvas holes in between, repeat the stitch pattern of the first column to give you two identical columns of stitches.

For the next column, the pattern changes.

- Bring the needle up at 13 and down at 14, across three bars, up at 15 and down at 16, again over three bars, up at 17 and down at 18, across four bars, up at 19 and down at 20, again over four bars, up at 21 and down at 22, across three bars.
- Leaving one bar of canvas in between, bring the needle up at 23 and down at 24, and mirror the stitches numbered 15–22.

The pattern changes again for the final column.

- Bring the needle up at 25 and down at 26, across five bars, up at 27 and down at 28, across six bars, up at 29 and down at 30, across four bars, up at 31 and down at 32, again over four bars, then mirror these stitches directly beneath.

Continue to work this four-column pattern until you have filled the desired area.

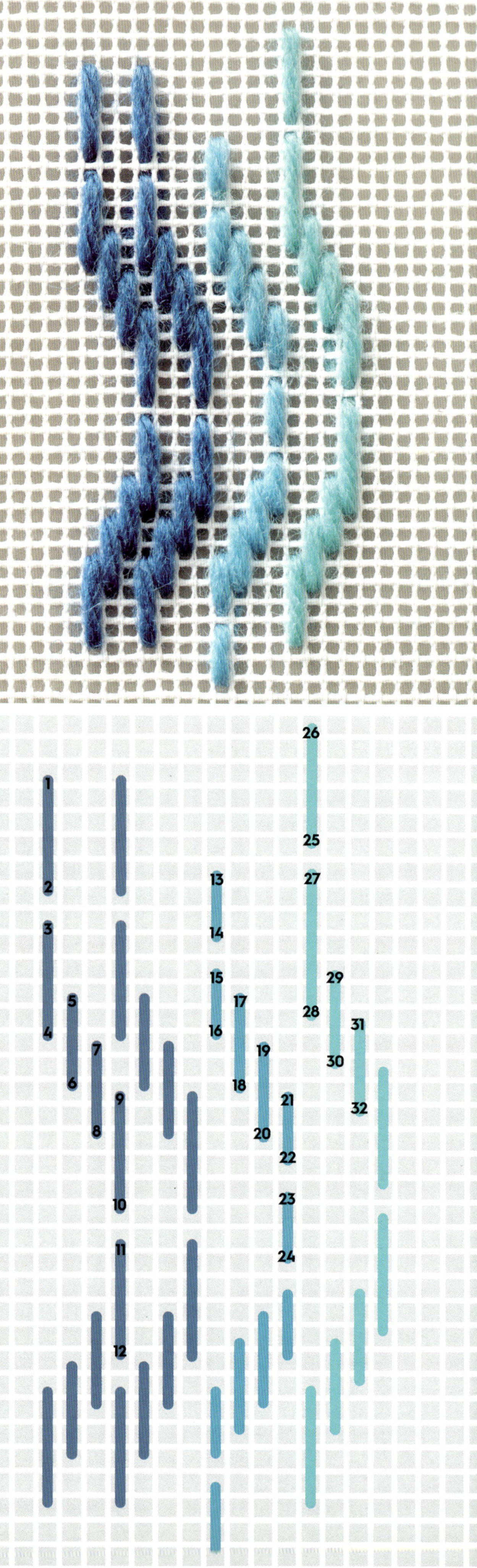

STICKS

The first time I saw this stitch I thought it looked like underwater plants, and then I started to see bubble trails, and so I knew it belonged here in the water section.

- Working from top to bottom, bring the needle up at 1 and down through the canvas hole at 2, across one intersection of canvas. Repeat to make a total of nine stitches, one beneath the other.
- Then bring the needle up at 5 and down at 6, across two intersections of canvas, and repeat to make a total of eight stitches, one beneath the other.
- To complete the stick stitch, bring the needle up at 9 and down at 10, across one intersection of canvas, aligning with the right-hand side of the stitches directly above, and repeat to make a total of nine stitches, one beneath the other.

Dot these stick stitch blocks around your canvas for best effect.

COLOUR CONFIDENCE

ONE OF THE JOYS OF NEEDLEPOINT FOR ME IS PLAYING WITH COLOUR. ALL YOU NEED IS A LITTLE CONFIDENCE! TAKE KITS, FOR EXAMPLE – MOST STITCHERS DILIGENTLY STICK TO THE THREADS PROVIDED, WHICH IS TOTALLY GREAT. AFTER ALL, THE DESIGNER HAS PUT TIME AND THOUGHT INTO THEIR COLOUR CHOICES. BUT WHAT IF YOU LOVE THE DESIGN BUT ONE OF THE COLOURS IS JUST TOO JARRING FOR YOU, OR THAT IF ONLY THE BACKGROUND WAS WORKED IN A DIFFERENT COLOUR, IT WOULD BE PERFECT FOR YOUR HOME?

MY TIP? REACH OUT TO THE KIT DESIGNER! YOU'D BE AMAZED HOW OPEN THEY WILL BE TO TWEAKING COLOURS FOR YOU. I'VE ALWAYS BEEN MET WITH A GIDDY DELIGHT THAT I'M ADDING MY OWN TWIST TO THE ORIGINAL. AFTER ALL, CREATIVE PEOPLE LOVE CREATIVE PEOPLE, AND ONE OF THE BEST THINGS ABOUT THIS COMMUNITY OF STITCHERS IS HOW WE LOVE TO CHEER EACH OTHER ON.

YOUR CHOICE OF COLOUR IS AS IMPORTANT AS YOUR CHOICE OF STITCH; IN MANY CASES THEY GO HAND IN HAND. TAKE DARNING HEARTS IN THE BORDERS SECTION AS AN EXAMPLE. YOU CAN CHOOSE CLASSIC REDS OR PINKS, OR SELECT A NEUTRAL WHITE TO LET THE TEXTURE AND SHAPE OF THE STITCH SPEAK FOR ITSELF, OR GO TOTALLY LEFT FIELD AND PICK A COLOUR THAT WOULD GIVE IT ANOTHER MEANING, SAY BLACK FOR A GOTH VIBE. SAME STITCH DIFFERENT ATMOSPHERE, AND ALL DONE WITH A SIMPLE CHANGE OF COLOUR.

LAND

SANDHILLS STITCH

This is ideal for stitching sweeping fields of grass, or long, sandy beaches, particularly if you work it in a variegated or textured thread.

+ Working the first column from top to bottom, bring the needle up at 1 and down through the canvas hole at 2, across four bars of canvas, up at 3 and down at 4, again across four bars. Continue in this way until you have a total of six four-bar stitches stepping down your canvas, as seen in the diagram.
+ Bring the needle up at 5 and down at 6, across two bars of canvas, and repeat two more times, stepping down each time.
+ Continue to repeat these long and short stitch steps until you have created a column filling the desired height.
+ Working the next column from bottom to top, bring the needle up at 9 and down at 10, alternating long and short stitch sets, and stepping up your canvas with each stitch.

CORNFIELD STITCH

The cornfield stitch looks just like corn sheaves stacked against each other.

+ Working from left to right, bring the needle up at 1 and down through the canvas hole at 2, across six bars of canvas, up 3 and down at 4, up at 5 and down at 6, up at 7 and down at 8, to stitch a set of four parallel vertical stitches.
+ You now have four parallel stitches all the same length. To work the belt in the centre of these stitches, bring the needle up through the canvas hole at 9 and down at 10.
+ To work the small sheaves in between the larger ones, bring the needle up at 11 and down at 12, across four bars of canvas, up at 13 and down at 14, and bring the needle up at 15 and down at 16 to cinch in this pair of shorter vertical stitches.
+ Continue in this way, alternating large and small corn sheaves, until you have a row filling the desired width.

On the next row, make sure to line up the different sizes of corn sheaves perfectly with each other.

GRASS SEED STITCH

I adapted this stitch when I was looking for a grass stitch that would work well in a small area of canvas. You'll find it's really easy to compensate too.

- Working from left to right, bring the needle up at 1 and down through the canvas hole at 2, across two bars of canvas at a slight diagonal.
- Bring the needle up at 3 and down at 4, across one intersection, to make a small diagonal stitch in the opposite direction.
- Bring the needle up at 5 (two canvas holes below 3) and down at 6, up at 7 and down at 8, to stagger your grass seed stitches.
- Continue to repeat these staggered grass seed stitches across your canvas.

RIDGE STITCH

Elongated cross stitches, tilted at an angle, have an amazing organic texture that is just perfect for stitching grass.

- Working from bottom to top, bring the needle up at 1 and down through the canvas hole at 2, across four bars of canvas at a slight diagonal. Bring the needle up at 3 and down at 4.

Notice how the start (1 and 3) and end (2 and 4) points of your stitches sit in holes diagonally next to each other.

- Bring the needle up two holes above 3 to start your next elongated cross stitch and continue until you have a column filling the desired height.
- Working the next column from top to bottom, bring the needle up at 5 and down at 6, up at 7 and down at 8.

Notice how the ends of your stitches sit in between the ends of the stitches in the previous column.

PERFECT PICNIC NAPKIN RINGS

BRING SOME SUMMER SUNSHINE TO YOUR TABLE ALL YEAR ROUND WITH THESE CUTE NAPKIN RINGS, USING DOUBLE V WITH UPRIGHT CROSSES TO CREATE A FLOWER MEADOW AND TRIPLE HUNGARIAN STITCH FOR FLUFFY CLOUDS. REFER TO THE MAKING UP SECTION FOR THE INSTRUCTIONS AND CHART FOR THIS PROJECT.

DOUBLE V WITH UPRIGHT CROSSES

This little flowery stitch is a lot of fun to play around with, especially if you add different colours to the upright crosses.

- Working from top to bottom for your first column, bring the needle up at 1 and down through the canvas hole at 2, across two intersections of canvas. Bring the needle up at 3 and down at 4 to create a perfect 'V'. Stitch a second 'V' directly above (5 to 6, 7 to 8) to create the double 'V'.
- Bring the needle up at 9 and down at 10, across two bars of canvas, and up at 11 and down at 12, again across two bars, to complete an upright cross stitch.

As you work your way up the column make sure that each part of the stitch aligns perfectly with the one below it.

- Working the next column, stagger your stitches as shown in the diagram.

GRASS STITCH

Here, long straight stitches create a strong horizon line, while small stitches share a canvas hole to give the impression of staggered tufts of grass.

Start at the left-hand side and work from bottom to top, to create a column of staggered pairs of horizontal stitches.

- Bring the needle up at 1 and down through the canvas hole at 2, across four bars of canvas, up at 3 and down at 4.
- Bring the needle up at 5 and down at 6, again across four bars of canvas, up at 7 and down at 8 to create your next pair of horizontal stitches, stepping up two bars to the right. Continue to work pairs of stitches in this way until you have a column filling the desired height.
- Now to work the tufts. Bring the needle up at 9 and down at 10, across one intersection, up at 11 and down at 10, across one bar, and up at 12 and down at 10, across one intersection. Continue in this way until each pair of horizontal stitches in the column has a tuft.
- Repeat these two columns until you have filled the desired area of the canvas.

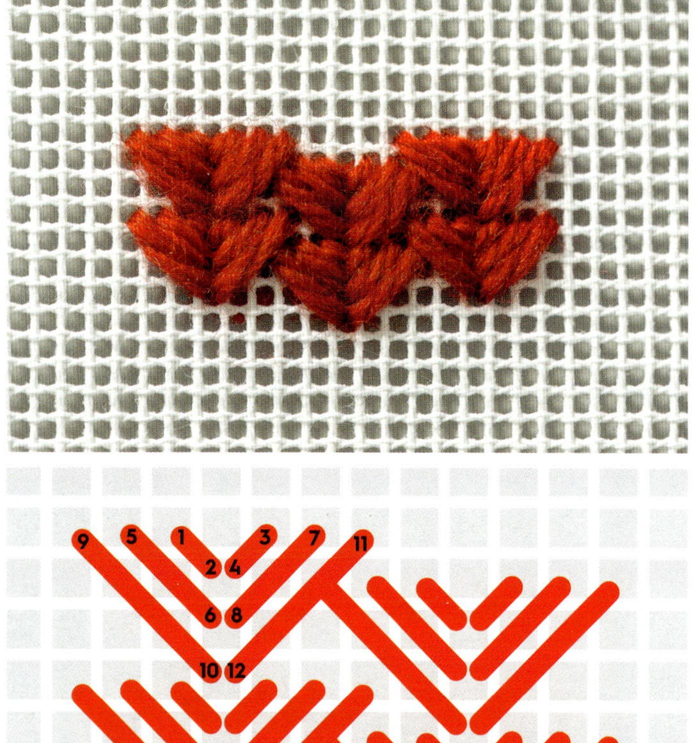

MILANESE STITCH VARIATION

Milanese stitches are always worked in triangular sections. This variation tilts them in towards each other to create lots of 'V's, giving the impression of leaves on trees or bushes.

- Working from top to bottom, bring the needle up at 1 and down through the canvas hole at 2, across one intersection. Bring the needle up at 3 and down at 4 to mirror the stitch.
- Bring the needle up at 5 and down at 6, across two intersections. Bring the needle up at 7 down at 8 to mirror the stitch.
- Bring the needle up at 9 and down at 10, across three intersections. Bring the needle up at 11 down at 12 to mirror the stitch.
- Continue in this way until you have a column filling the desired height.
- For your next column, start one set of holes down, and stagger each column as seen in the diagram.

REVERSE BRICK STITCH

If you were to look under your canvas when stitching brick stitch, this is what you would see. It's far too pretty to be hidden beneath, so it's time for its moment in the spotlight.

- Working from left to right, bring the needle up at 1 and down through the canvas hole at 2, across one intersection of canvas. Bring the needle up at 3 and down at 4, across three bars of canvas at a slight diagonal. Continue in this way until you have a row filling the desired width.
- Working the next row from right to left, bring the needle up at 5 and down at 6, up at 7 and down at 8, to tilt your stitches in the opposite direction from the row above.

The long stitches should line up with the short stitches and vice versa.

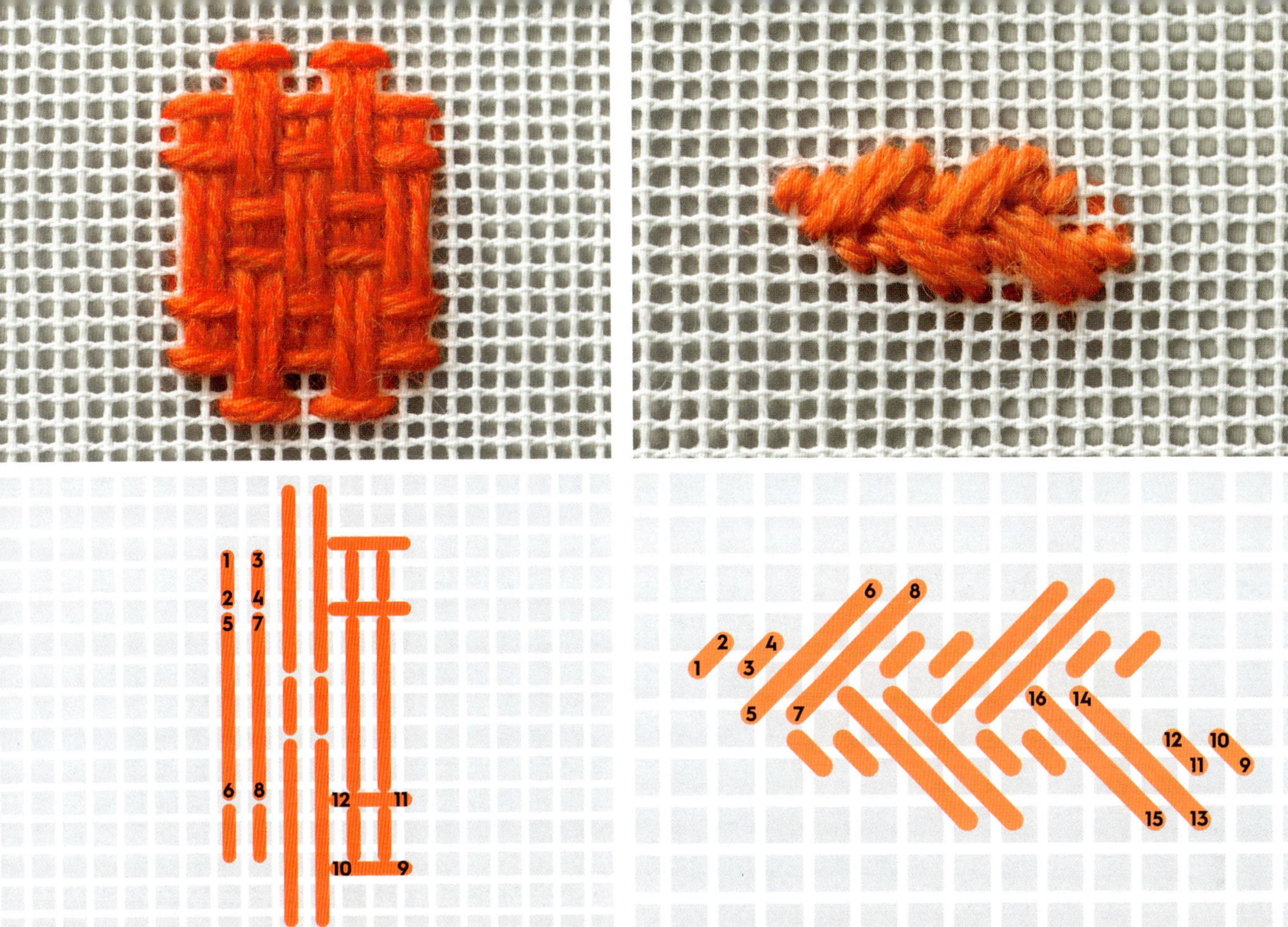

BAMBOO STITCH

With its really long stitch sections, this is best used for large areas of canvas where a tall design is called for.

Start by stitching all the vertical stitches first.

+ Working from top to bottom, bring the needle up at 1 and down through the canvas hole at 2, across two bars of canvas. Bring the needle up at 3 and down at 4, to make a parallel stitch.
+ Bring the needle up at 5 and down at 6, across six bars of canvas, and up at 7 and down at 8, to make a parallel stitch. Continue in this way until you have a column filling the desired height.
+ Work the next column from bottom to top, so that the pairs of small vertical stitches are positioned centrally to the long stitches in the column before. Continue in this way until you have filled the desired width.

Now to create the distinctive ridges along your bamboo lengths.

+ Bring the needle up at 9 and down at 10, across three bars of canvas, then up at 11 and down at 12; continue to work horizontal stitches at the ends of the vertical stitches (diagram shows this in progress).

DOUBLE ALTERNATING NOBUKO STITCH

I love the zigzag nature of this stitch and I find it works equally well for stitching trees, shrubs and grass.

+ Working from left to right, bring the needle up at 1 and down through the canvas hole at 2, across one intersection of canvas. Bring the needle up at 3 and down at 4, to make a parallel stitch.
+ Bring the needle up at 5 and down at 6, across three intersections of canvas, and bring the needle up at 7 and down at 8, to make a parallel stitch. Continue to work pairs of stitches in this way until you have a row filling the desired width.
+ Working from right to left for the next row, continue to stitch alternating pairs of short and long stitches, but this time tilted in the opposite direction, as shown in the diagram.

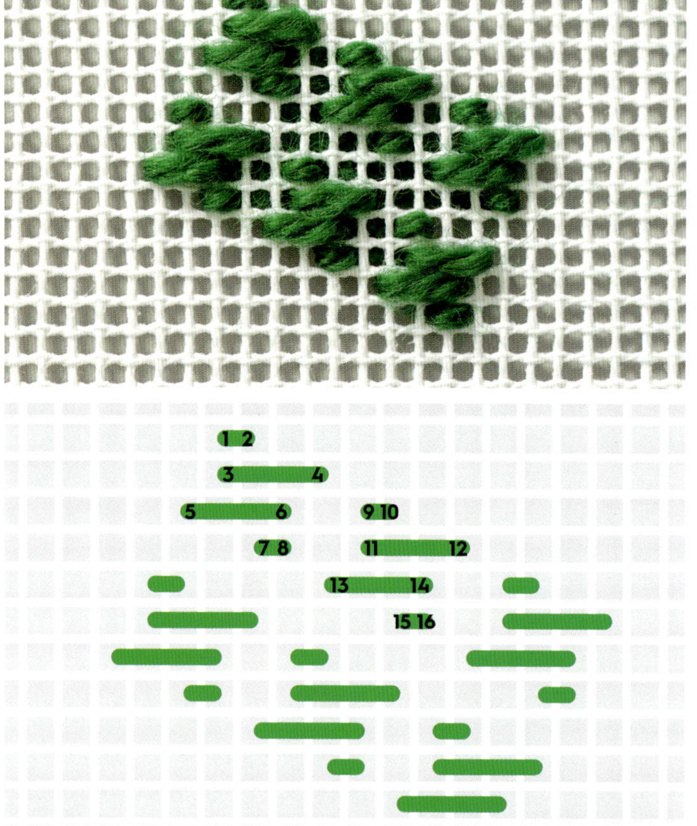

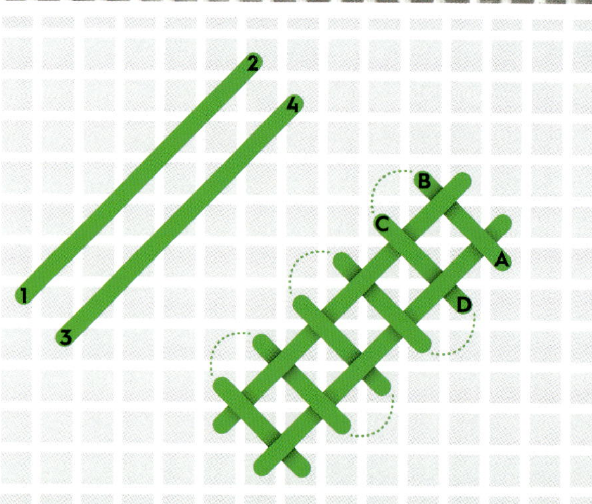

DIAGONAL CHECKS

The structure of these stitch blocks and the space they have around make them a contender for a textured thread. They can give the illusion of shrubbery, grass ridges, sand dunes, or maybe even snow peaks.

Starting at the left-hand side of your work, stitch each of the check blocks from top to bottom, to form diagonal rows across the canvas.

- Bring the needle up at 1 and down through the canvas hole at 2, across one bar of canvas. Bring the needle up at 3 and down at 4, across three bars, up at 5 and down at 6, across three bars. Bring the needle up at 7 and down at 8, across one bar.
- To start the next check block, bring the needle up at 9 and down at 10 and continue as before.

Notice that there is a one-hole gap between the third and fourth stitches of your first block and the first and second stitches of your next block.

- Continue in this way until you have filled the desired area.

NEEDLE WEAVING

This makes beautiful hedge borders. It can be worked at any angle, diagonal, vertical or horizontal, as the method for weaving stays the same regardless.

First, work the stitches that form the warp for the weave. These can be as long as you dare them to be, but I've worked mine across six intersections of the canvas.

- Bring the needle up at 1 and down through the canvas hole at 2, and up at 3 and down at 4 to make a parallel stitch.

Now weave your needle in and out of the warp lengths.

- Bring the needle up through the canvas hole at A and take it over one warp thread and under the other warp thread to bring it down at B.
- Bring the needle up through the canvas hole at C and take it over one warp thread and under the other warp thread to bring it down at D.
- Continue in this way, alternating the weave as shown in the diagram (the dotted line shows the journey of your weaving thread under the canvas).

DIAMOND RAY STITCH

This pretty little stitch is a great addition to any canvas and works well scattered randomly about a project either for little shrubs or tufts of grass.

+ Bring the needle up at 1 and down through the canvas hole at 2, across three bars of canvas at a slight diagonal.
+ Bring the needle up at 3 and down at 2, up at 4 and down at 2, up at 5 and down at 2.

Notice how each of these stitches start in the hole diagonally above the start point of the previous stitch.

+ Now that you have reached the apex of your diamond, mirror your stitches back down. Bring the needle up at 6 and down at 2, up at 7 and down at 2, up at 8 and down at 2.

TEXTURED THREADS

IF YOU'RE LOOKING TO EXPERIMENT WITH THE WORLD OF TEXTURED STITCHES, THEN TEXTURED THREADS ARE A REALLY EXCITING AREA TO EXPLORE. FLUFFY ONES, STRAW-LIKE ONES, FROSTY ONES THAT LOOK LIKE ICE WHEN STITCHED. BASICALLY, IF YOU HAVE A TEXTURE YOU WANT YOUR STITCHING TO EMULATE, THEN THERE'S BOUND TO BE A THREAD OUT THERE READY TO HELP.

IMAGINE USING LONG UPRIGHT CROSS STITCH IN A FUZZY THREAD FOR THE WOOLLY FLEECE OF A SHEEP, WOULDN'T THAT LOOK CUTE? OR WHAT ABOUT A FROSTY THREAD TO CREATE SNOWFLAKE STITCH ON A WINTRY DESIGN?

EVEN IF YOU'RE STRICTLY BASKETWEAVING YOUR WAY ACROSS A CANVAS, MAYBE YOU COULD EXPERIMENT WITH THREAD TEXTURES TO ADD A NEW DYNAMIC TO THE FINISH? I ONCE USED A FUZZY THREAD PURELY IN A TENT STITCH FOR AN AREA OF CARPET ON A CANVAS, AND IT WAS PERFECTION!

GET CREATIVE AND DON'T BE AFRAID TO EXPERIMENT. TAKE A WANDER AROUND YOUR LOCAL NEEDLEPOINT STORE AND SEE WHICH THREADS CATCH YOUR EYE. WHAT ARE YOU WAITING FOR...?

BORDERS

DARNING HEARTS

An excellent border for a valentine project, these staggered satin stitch hearts seem to burst across the canvas.

+ Working from left to right, bring the needle up at 1 and down through the canvas hole at 2, across three bars of canvas. Bring the needle up at 3 and down at 4, across five bars, then up at 5 and down at 6, this time going across six bars of canvas. For the mid-point of your heart shape, bring the needle up at 7 and down at 8, across six bars of canvas, then mirror the shape of the first half of your stitches to complete your first heart.
+ To start your next heart, bring the needle up at 9 and down at 10, across three bars of canvas and continue as before.

Notice how the three-bar starting stitch of one heart lines up with the finishing or starting three-bar stitch of the heart above or below it.

SNOWFLAKE STITCH

Line up your snowflake stitches to trim those wintertime makes, using a fuzzy or metallic thread if you choose to, for a winter wonderland vibe.

+ Bring the needle up at 1 and down at 2, across four bars of canvas, then up at 3 and down at 4, again across four bars. Bring the needle up at 5 and down at 6, across two intersections of canvas, then up at 7 and down at 8. This creates the star shape at the centre of your snowflake.

Now you are going to add a little fork to the ends of each of the diagonal stitches of the centre star.

+ Bring the needle up at 9 and down at 10, across two bars of canvas, then up at 11 and down at 9, again across two bars, then up at 12 and down at 9, across two intersections of the canvas. Continue in this way around the centre star as shown in the diagram.

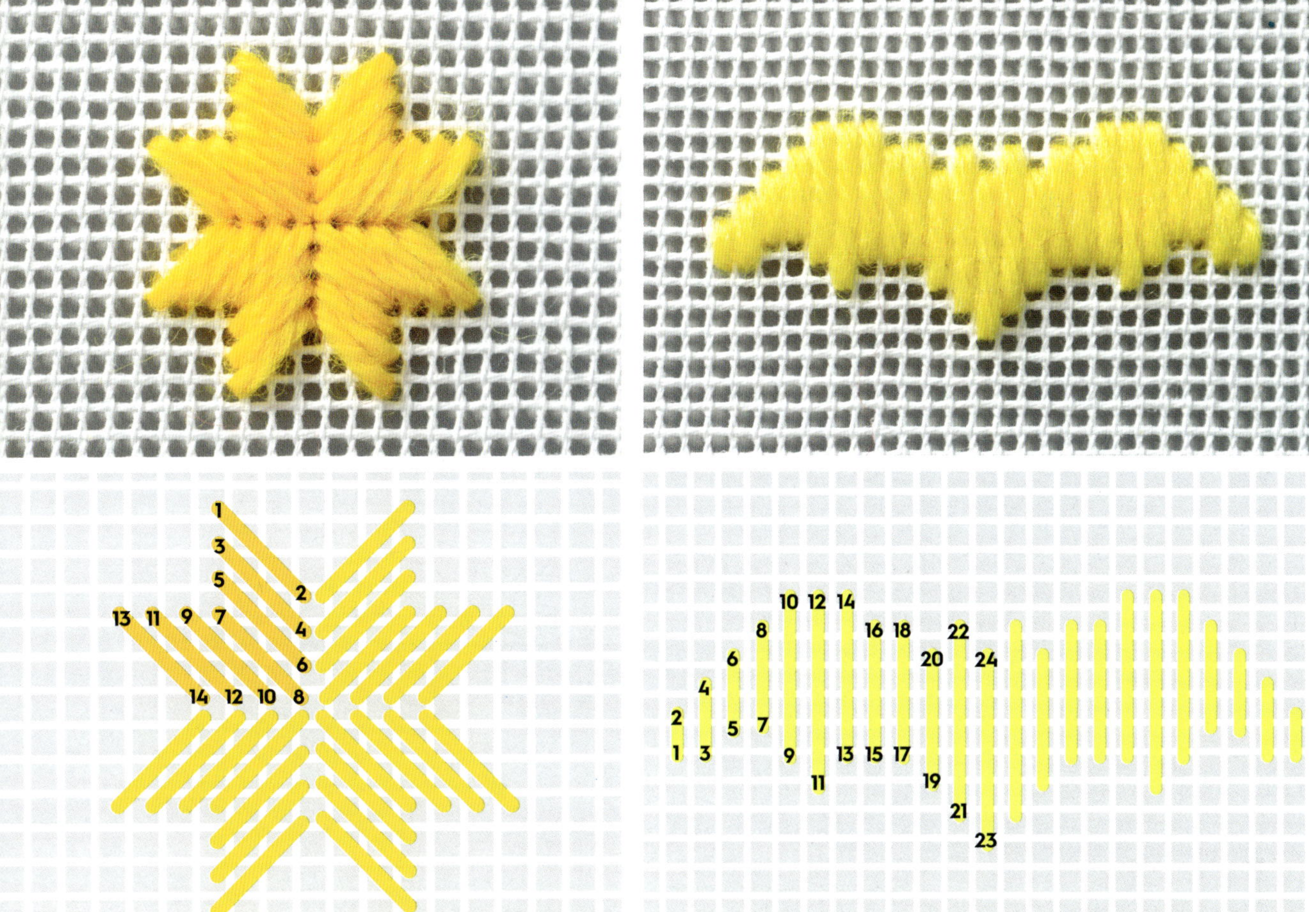

SATIN STITCH STAR

The puffy sheen of satin stitch makes this border motif stand out on wintry night-time designs.

- Bring the needle up at 1 and down through the canvas hole at 2, across three intersections. Bring the needle up at 3 and down at 4, up at 5 and down at 6, up at 7 and down at 8, to make a total of four parallel diagonal stitches.
- Moving one hole to the side, bring the needle up at 9 and down at 10, up at 11 and down at 12, up at 13 and down at 14, across three intersections of canvas, as shown in the diagram. This completes one quarter of the star.
- Turn your canvas 90-degrees clockwise and repeat to stitch the second quarter of the star. Continue in this way until you have worked a full star as shown in the diagram.

BAT MOTIF

If you love the spooky season, or even winged superheroes, this makes the perfect border!

For this motif vertical stitches are worked to different lengths, sometimes moving up or down by one canvas hole, so follow the stitch diagram carefully to capture the distinctive bat silhouette.

- Working from left to right, bring the needle up at 1 and down through the canvas hole at 2, across two bars of canvas. Bring the needle up at 3 and down at 4, across three bars, then up at 5 and down at 6, again across three bars. Now bring the needle up at 7 and down at 8, this time across four bars to form the tip of the wing.
- Bring the needle up at 9 and down at 10, across six bars, up at 11 and down at 12, across seven bars, up at 13 and down at 14, this time across six bars. Notice how these three stitches align at the top to create the apex of the wing.
- Now working in towards the body of the bat, bring the needle up at 15 and down at 16, across five bars, up at 17 and down at 18, across five bars, up at 19 and down at 20, across five bars, up at 21 and down at 22, across seven bars.
- Bring the needle up at 23 and down at 24, across seven bars, for the centre length of the bat's body, then simply mirror your stitches to complete the bat motif.

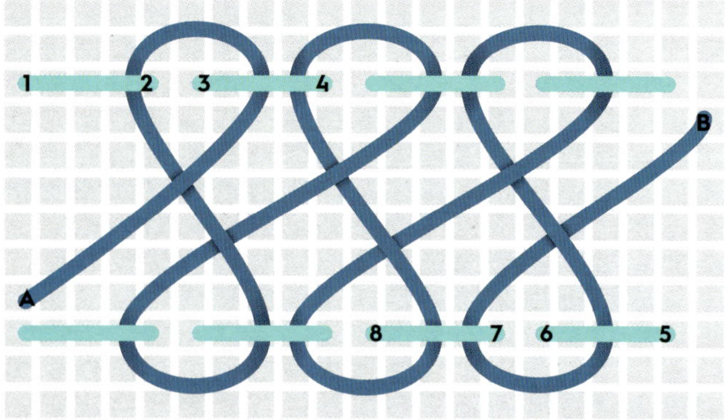

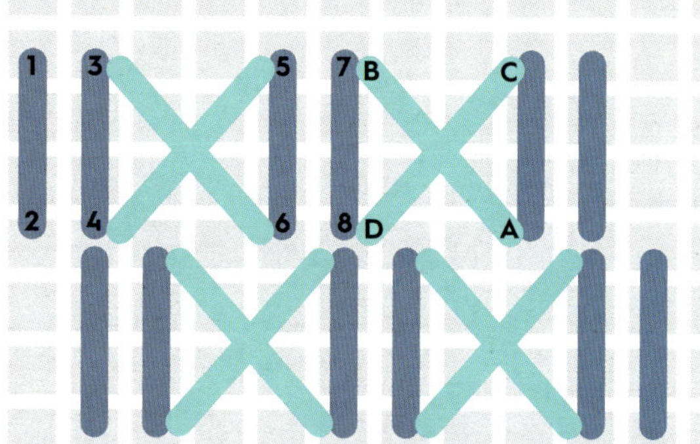

INTERLACING STITCH

When I first tried this stitch I found it a little tricky, but with practice you get into a great rhythm and you'll be mastering it in no time.

- Bring the needle up at 1 and down at 2, across four bars of canvas, and up at 3 and down at 4, again across four bars, so there is one bar space between each stitch. Continue in this way until you have a row of stitches filling the desired width.
- Leaving six empty holes in between rows, start the next row with a new length of thread to avoid travelling. Bring the needle up at 5 and down at 6, across four bars, and continue to work a row of stitches parallel to the first row.

Now selecting a different colour of thread, interlace it through the top and bottom rows of horizontal stitches.

- Bring the needle up at A and weave your thread in and out of the stitches of the top and bottom rows, carefully following the sequence shown in the diagram, finally bringing it back down through the canvas at B.

ROMAN CROSS

This structured border stitch, with its Roman numeral appearance, is great worked in a single row, or as off-centred rows as I've stitched here.

- Working from left to right, bring the needle up at 1 and down through the canvas hole at 2, across three bars of canvas, then up at 3 and down at 4, again across three bars. Leaving two holes of canvas in between, bring the needle up at 5 and down at 6, up at 7 and down at 8 to create another pair of stitches. Continue in this way until you have a row of stitches filling the desired width.

Now to add a cross stitch in between each pair of vertical stitches.

- Bring the needle up at A and down at B, across three intersections, and up at C and down at D to complete the cross.

LITTLE TREASURES TRINKET TRAY

WITH ITS DISTINCTIVE ROMAN CROSS EDGES AND BASE PANEL WORKED IN PUFFY PADDED BALLOON STITCH, THIS IS THE PERFECT PLACE TO KEEP YOUR JEWELLERY SAFELY TO HAND. REFER TO THE MAKING UP SECTION FOR THE INSTRUCTIONS AND CHART FOR THIS PROJECT.

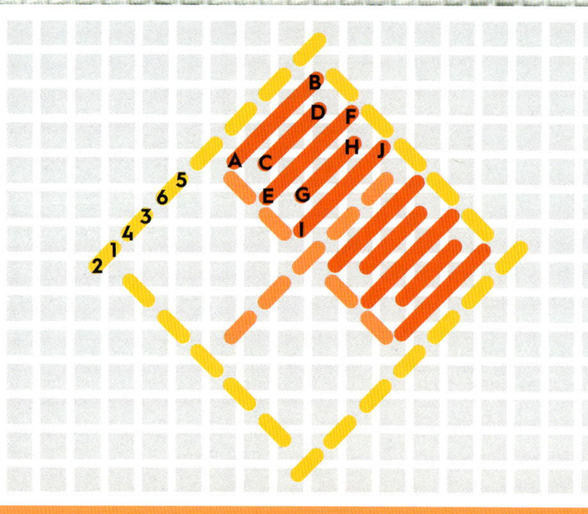

ALTERNATING SCOTCH SQUARES WITH LAYERED OBLIQUE CROSSES

Decorative in its own right, this makes a gorgeous border stitch. Play with thread colours to accentuate its flowery shape.

- First, stitch the blocks of alternating Scotch squares that form the corner sections of the large squares. Bring the needle up at 1 and down through the canvas hole at 2, across one intersection, up at 3 and down at 4, across two intersections, up at 5 and down at 6, across three intersections. Decreasing stitch lengths, bring the needle up at 7 and down at 8, up at 9 and down at 10. Turn 90-degrees clockwise and repeat. Continue to work all four corners.
- Skipping one bar, repeat and continue until you have a row filling the desired width. For a wider border, work a single row of alternating Scotch squares below, so the squares share corner blocks for a staggered effect, as shown.
- Now to stitch the layered oblique cross detail. Bring the needle up at A and down at B, across five bars of canvas at a slight diagonal, then up at C and down at D to form the vertical arm of the cross. Then bring the needle up at E and down at F, and up at G and down at H, working as before to form the horizontal arm.

ARGYLE STITCH

This is best worked in three colours to emphasize the Argyle pattern for which it is named.

- First stitch the outer diamond, shown in yellow. Bring the needle up at 1 and down through the canvas hole at 2, across one intersection, up at 3 and down at 4, up at 5 and down at 6. Continue on this line until you have a row of seven stitches. Work the remaining lines that form the outer diamond, so you have two parallel sides of seven stitches, and two of five stitches.
- Then stitch the infill stitches, shown in red, in the centre of the diamond. Bring the needle up at A and down at B, across three intersections, up at C and down at D, across two intersections. Repeat (E/F and G/H), then bring the needle up at I and down at J, across three intersections. Skip a row of intersections and repeat the block.
- Work two more blocks of infill stitches to the left, making sure that the long stitches of these blocks share a canvas hole with the long stitches in the first two blocks.
- Now fill in your internal crosslines to complete the Argyle stitch pattern, as shown in pink.

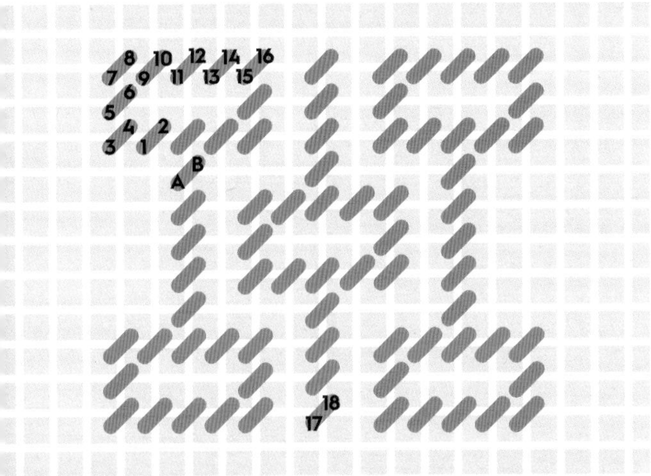

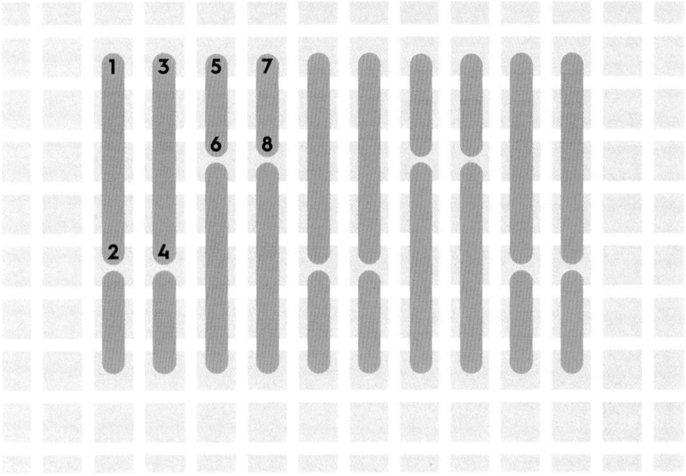

MOD SCREEN

This super easy border is worked entirely with tent stitches; its shape echoes the modern screen designs of the seventies.

Remember to work your tent stitches over one intersection of canvas throughout.

+ Bring the needle up at 1 and down at 2, up at 3 and down at 4. Stepping up, bring the needle up at 5 and down at 6, up at 7 and down at 8. Stepping right, bring the needle up at 9 and down at 10 and continue to form the top line (five stitches in a horizontal row). Continue to complete the rectangle at the top of the column.
+ Locate the centre stitch at the bottom of the rectangle and, bringing the needle up at A and down at B, work a vertical line of five stitches beneath. Then work another rectangle at the base of this line, as before.
+ For the next part of the pattern start a new thread. Bring the needle up at 17 and down at 18, stitching a vertical row of four stitches, then top it with a rectangular block, worked as before, and complete with another row of four stitches.
+ Continue to repeat these two columns until you reach the desired width.

NITE KNOTTERS

This is the perfect stitch to play with colours to try out lots of different effects. It's very easy to work around any project's border.

+ Working from left to right, bring the needle up at 1 and down through the canvas hole at 2, across four bars of canvas, then up at 3 and down at 4.
+ Bring the needle up at 5 and down at 6, across two bars of canvas, then up at 7 and down at 8.
+ Repeat these pairs of long and short vertical stitches and continue until you have a row filling the desired width.
+ For the next row, work from right to left, lining up the pairs of longer stitches with the shorter stitches and vice versa.

CUTE CARD KEEPER WALLET

SOMETIMES A BORDER STITCH IS JUST THE THING WHEN YOU'RE LOOKING TO ADD AN EYE-CATCHING BAND – HERE, SHADOW MESH FITS THE BILL PERFECTLY! SPEAKING OF BILLS, THIS HANDY WALLET WILL BE THE ENVY OF YOUR FRIENDS. REFER TO THE MAKING UP SECTION FOR THE INSTRUCTIONS AND CHART FOR THIS PROJECT.

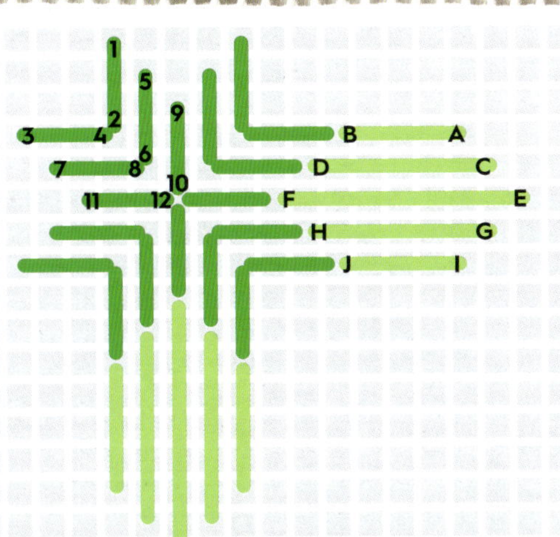

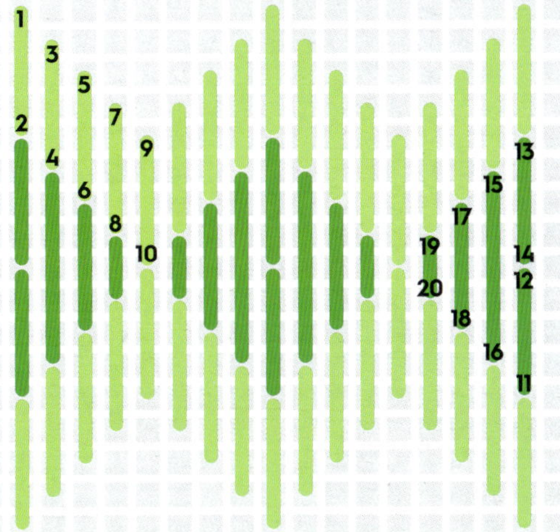

FRAMING STITCH

Sometimes all your project needs is decorative corners rather than a full-blown border. Here's one, with a hint of the Art Deco about it for you to try.

- Bring the needle up at 1 and down through the canvas hole at 2, across three bars of canvas, and up at 3 and down at 4 to create a right angle. Stepping one hole down to the right, bring the needle up at 5 and down at 6, up at 7 and down at 8, across three bars of canvas each time. One more step down and make another right-angle bringing the needle up at 9 and down at 10, up at 11 and down at 12.
- Turning your canvas 90-degrees clockwise each time, repeat the stitch sequence 1 to 12 to create a full star as shown in the diagram, and stitch this full-star motif in each corner of your canvas.
- Now add straight stitches to the inner arms of the star motifs at the length of your choice. If you follow my stitching pattern (marked A to J on the diagram), your corner motif will have a glamorous thirties vibe.

SHADOW MESH

This is a big bold border stitch, and I love it so much that I made it the feature stitch on my Cute Card Keeper Wallet project!

- Working from left to right, bring the needle up at 1 and down through the canvas hole at 2, across four bars of canvas. Stepping down one hole to the right each time, bring the needle up at 3 and down at 4, up at 5 and down at 6, up at 7 and down at 8, up at 9 and down at 10. Now, stepping up one hole to the right each time, make vertical stitches across four bars of canvas as shown on the diagram. Continue in this way until your zigzagging row of stitches fills the desired width.

If you are using two colours, as I have in the stitch sample, now is a great time to park your thread.

- Now to work the middle section between the top and bottom zigzagging rows. Bring the needle up 11 and down at 12 across four bars of canvas, then up at 13 and down at 14. Bring the needle up at 15 and down at 16, across six bars, then up at 17 and down at 18, across four bars, and up at 19 and down at 20, across two bars.

Once you have completed your middle section, take up your first colour once again and complete the bottom zigzag as before.

RHODES CIRCLE

If you are looking for more of a 3D detail for your border, Rhodes circle creates beautifully puffy polka dots!

+ Bring the needle up at 1 and down through the canvas hole at 2, across seven bars of canvas at a slight diagonal.
+ Bring your needle up at 3 and down at 4, and continue working in a clockwise direction to form the circular shape. Carefully count how many bars and intersections each stitch covers to ensure you achieve the correct shape.
+ Bring your needle up at 27 and down at 28 to complete the Rhodes circle.

PINS AND NEEDLES STITCH

I was looking for the perfect stitch to celebrate my love of needlepoint, so I took to my sketch book and came up with a cute border that spotlights the tools of my trade.

+ Bring the needle up at 1 and down through the canvas hole at 2, across one bar of canvas, up at 3 and down at 4, up at 5 and down at 6, up at 7 and down at 8, to create a little square of stitches to make the head of the pin. Then bring the needle up at 9 and down at 10, across five intersections of canvas, to make the length of the pin.
+ Leaving two holes in between, bring the needle up at 11 and down at 12, and up at 13 and down at 14, across two intersections of canvas, to make the eye of the needle. Then bring the needle up at 15 and down at 16, across five intersections of canvas, to make the length of the needle.

DOUBLE DOUBLED CROSS STITCH

A big bold stitch, this can be grouped together for a strong defined border or worked singly just at the corners.

- Bring the needle up at 1 and down through the canvas hole at 2, across seven bars of canvas at a slight diagonal, then up at 3 and down at 4.
- Bring the needle up at 5 and down at 6, again across seven bars of canvas at a slight diagonal, then up at 7 and down at 8.

This is a variation on an upright cross stitch. Now work the doubled cross stitch over it.

- Bring the needle up at 9 and down at 10, across six intersections of canvas, then up at 11 and down at 12. Bring the needle up at 13 and down at 14, again across six intersections of canvas, then up at 15 and down at 16.
- To highlight the corners of the top cross stitch, work a small diagonal stitch across two intersections of the canvas at each corner, bringing the needle up at A and down at B as shown on the diagram.

VERTICAL SPLIT SATIN

The height of this border stitch is easily adjusted by increasing the number of stitch lengths. Here I've worked it in single blocks, lining them up with a little space in between.

- Bring your needle up through the canvas hole at 1 and down at 2, up at 3 and down at 4, up at 5 and down at 6, across four intersections each time.
- Then bring your needle up at 7 and down at 8, this time across two intersections, and up at 9 and down at 10, again across two intersections. Repeat directly beneath, up at 11 and down at 12, up at 13 and down at 14, and then up at 15 and down at 16, up at 17 and down at 18.
- Complete your vertical split satin column by stitching three more stitches over four intersections, as shown in the diagram.
- Continue to stitch vertical split satin columns in this way until you have a row of stitches filling the desired width.

You can choose to line columns up perfectly next to each other, leaving two bars of canvas space in between, as shown in the diagram, or experiment with connecting them, or staggering them (as shown in the stitched sample).

MAKING UP INSTRUCTIONS

BIRDS AND BLOSSOMS BANNER

Welcome nature into your makes with this beautiful design and celebrate a wonderful variety of dynamic and textural stitches as you do so! The bodies of the parakeets are stitched in simple tent stitch, but it's the stitches I have chosen for their tail and wing feathers that really animates them. You'll see how even a simple stitch like chopsticks can suddenly bring a bloom to life, and a swirl stitch background seems to launch our feathered friends into the sky.

01 The best place to start this design is by working the branches in the bottom right-hand corner in tent stitch (see photo 1), then their blossoms. This provides a great anchor point for you to count in the rest of your pattern. Referring to chart 1, count up from the bottom right-hand corner of your canvas and cast on.

02 When stitching the blossoms, stitch their maroon centres first in tent stitch, then the petal areas. I alternated stitching tent stitch flower blooms with those worked with chopsticks and the good news is, both of these stitches are easy to compensate! If you fancy trying this too, just pick a bloom every now and then and stitch it in chopsticks. If your flower shape changes slightly from the chart, don't worry – it'll make the design uniquely yours!

YOU WILL NEED

- One 27 x 34cm (10⅝ x 13⅜in) sheet of 10-ct plastic canvas
- Anchor Tapestry Wool: three skeins of colour 8872 (light blue); one skein each of colours 8400 (maroon), 8362 (pale pink), 8254 (peach), 8006 (white), 9450 (dark brown), 9488 (light brown), 8988 (dark green), 9096 (light green), 8454 (bright pink), 8394 (light pink), 9800 (black), 8118 (dark yellow) and 8092 (light yellow)
- Size 20 tapestry needle
- Embroidery scissors

STITCHES USED

Basics Tent stitch.

Movement Staggered half diamond ray stitch; Wing stitch; Italic stitch.

Texture Chopsticks.

Sky Swirl stitch.

CHART 1

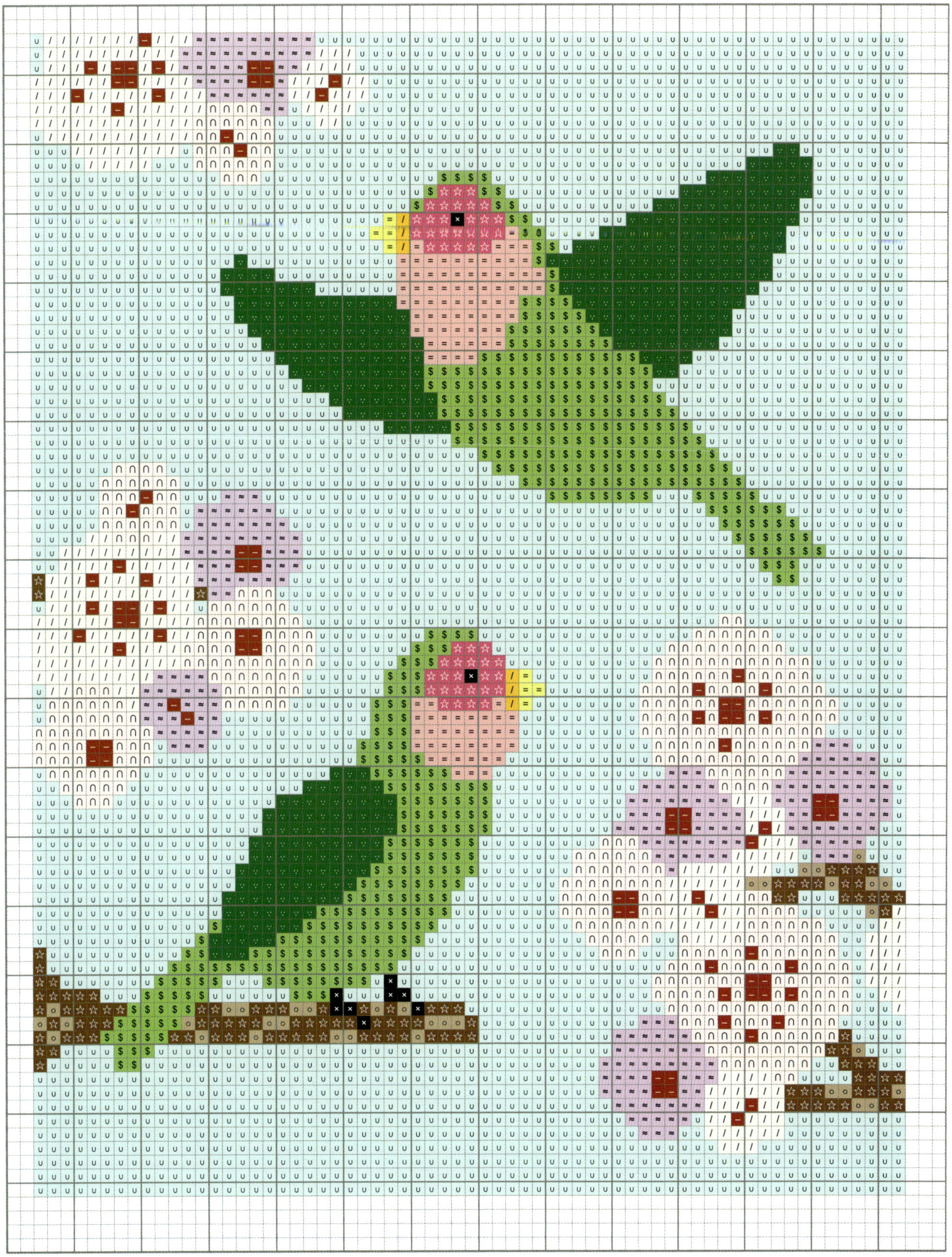

8006	8362	8400	8254	8988	8394	9096
8454	8118	9800	8092	9450	8872	9488

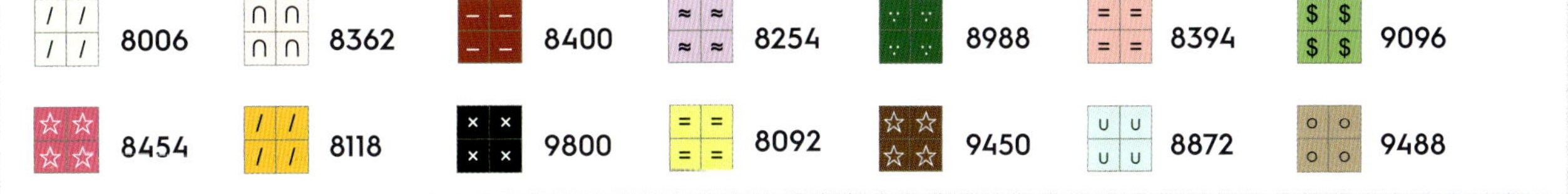

03 Next, move on to stitch the body, head and tail of each of the birds, leaving the wings for now. The body and head are stitched in simple tent stitch and the tail in italic stitch, which really captures the rigidity of the tail feathers (see photo 2). I've outlined the exact stitching of the tails in chart 2 to give you a helping hand.

04 The bird wings are the trickiest part of this design! I've chosen staggered half diamond ray stitch for the perched bird and wing stitch with filling tent stitches for the bird in flight. I've shown the stitch placement on chart 2 but I also have a handy tip for how to tackle filling an area of blank canvas with a decorative stitch, as illustrated in photo 3. Outline the area to be filled with tent stitches, worked in a bright contrasting colour. This way, you can fill the area with confidence, as you can easily see where to stop your compensating stitches. When you're done, just carefully unpick the outlining stitches.

05 Now all that remains is to fill in the background with swirl stitch. The easiest place to start is in the bottom left-hand corner to give yourself a clear run to establish the shape.

06 Once the stitching is complete, it's time to trim your plastic canvas, leaving one bar of canvas all the way around the edge (see photo 4).

07 To make a hanging cord for the banner, cut a 30cm (12in) length from your remaining wool, thread it through the top corners from the back of your canvas and tie a knot at each end (see photo 5).

CHART 2

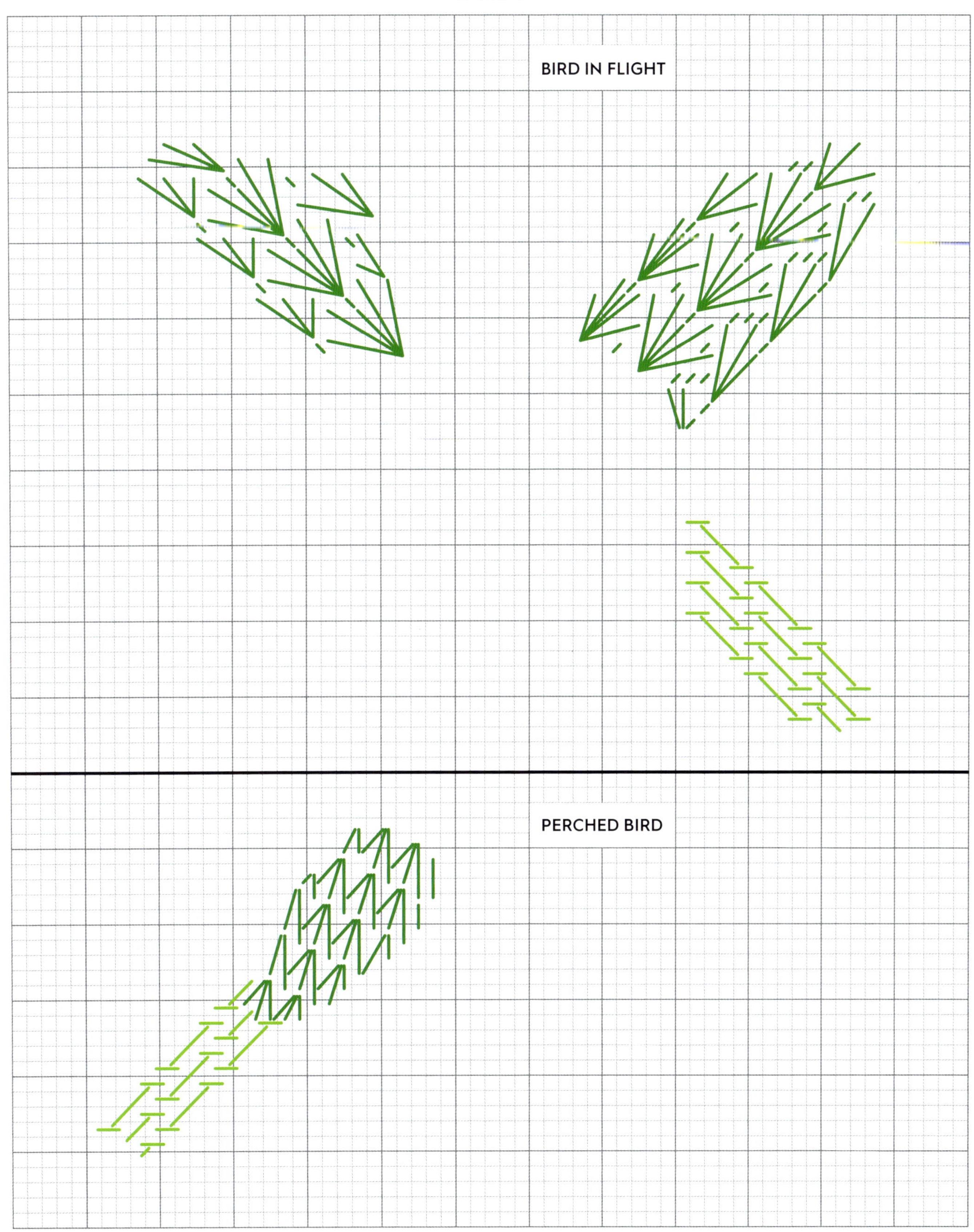

SWEET AND SIMPLE CAKE FLAGS

Cakes have never looked so good as when decorated with a celebratory set of cake flags! Quick and easy, this is the perfect customizable project. Each flag is stitched with just one stitch from this collection, and I've chosen a few of my favourites to showcase how you can simply build beautiful patterns with them. I've used my preferred candy colours, but feel free to change your colour palette to suit the occasion.

---

01 Refer to the charts for how to stitch the flags as shown and this is also a useful guide for how to space them out on the plastic canvas sheet. If you are working from the edge of the canvas as I have in photo 1, remember to start one bar of canvas from the edge. It's totally up to you how you want to mix and match your colours, and you can substitute stitches of your own choosing to make your cake flags. Stitch each flag design twice to make a front and back panel.

YOU WILL NEED

- One 27 x 34cm (10⅝ x 13⅜in) sheet of 10-ct plastic canvas
- Anchor Tapestry Wool: one skein each of colours 8002 (white), 8962 (mint), 8432 (dark pink) 8392 (light pink), 8590 (dark purple), 8586 (light purple) and 8092 (light yellow)
- DMC Stranded Cotton (floss): one skein of colour 964 (mint)
- Size 20 tapestry needle
- Size 6 to 8 embroidery needle
- Embroidery scissors
- Bamboo barbecue skewers

STITCHES USED

Texture Balloon stitch; Condensed cashmere stitch variation; Double woven stitch.

Water Mini wave stitch.

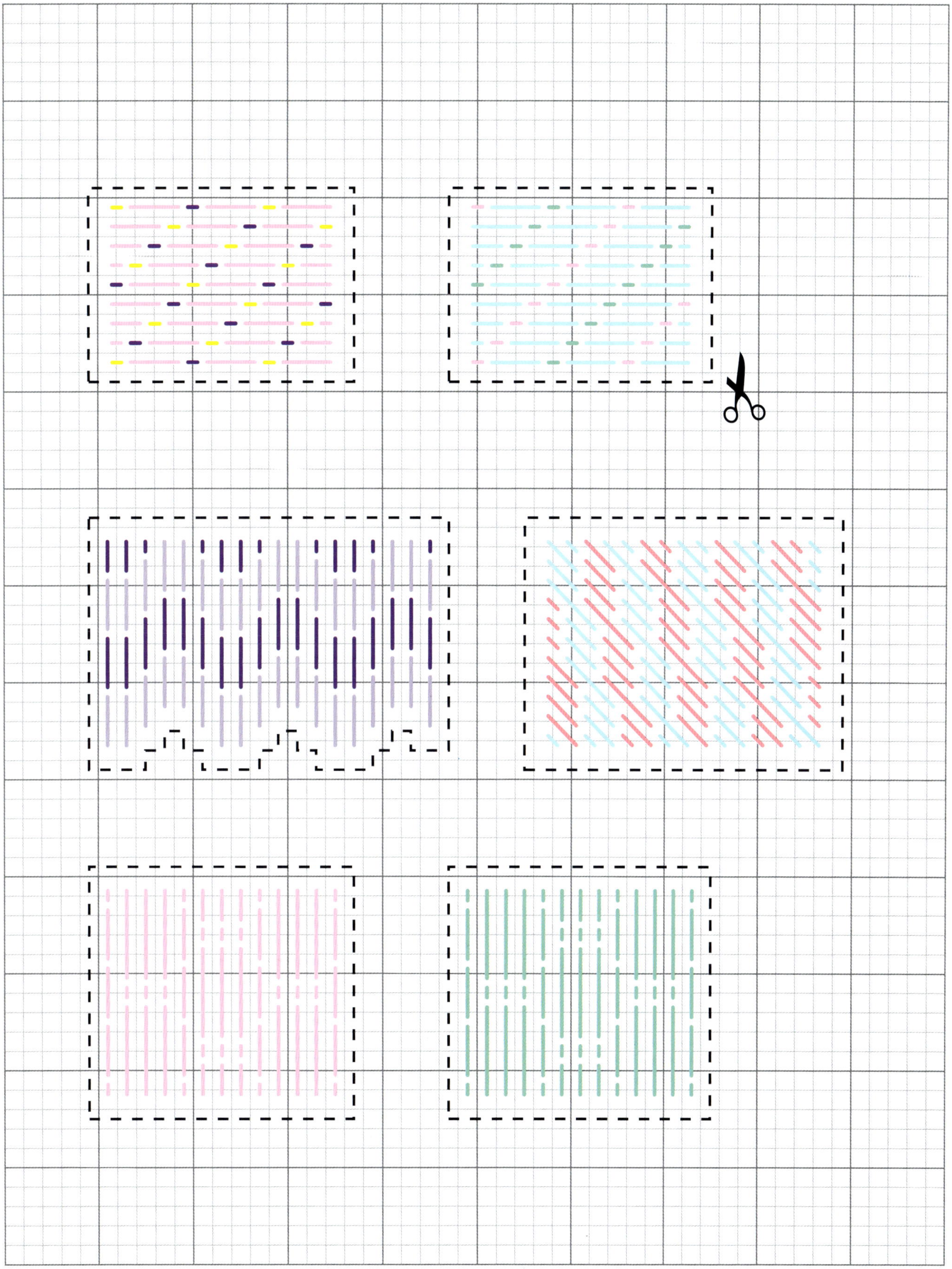

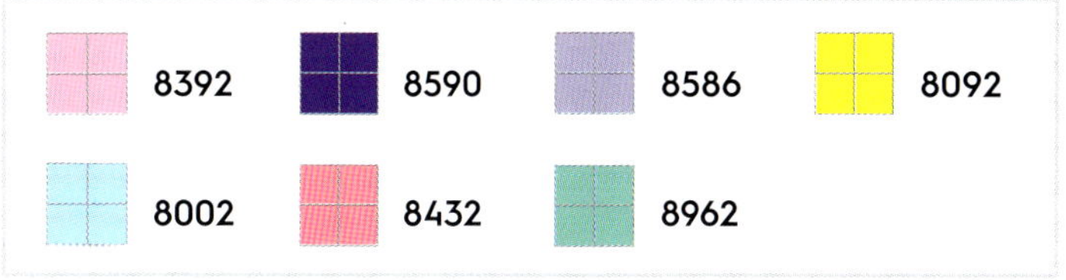
8392
8590
8586
8092
8002
8432
8962

02 Once the stitching is complete, it's time to trim your plastic canvas, leaving one bar of canvas all the way around the edge (see photo 2).

03 Thread the embroidery needle with a length of stranded cotton (floss), just one strand is perfect, and pairing up the front and back panels of each flag, start joining them together with a simple running stitch. Beginning at the left-hand side, bring your needle up and down the edge of the canvas, working along the top and down the right-hand side, but leaving the bottom edge of the flag panels unsewn for now (photo 3).

04 Trim off the top section of the barbecue skewers by gently scoring them with a pair of craft scissors (see photo 4), then give them a snap. Trim off any sharp bits.

TO GIVE YOUR FLAGS MORE IMPACT, CUT YOUR SKEWERS AT DIFFERENT HEIGHTS.

05 Place the trimmed edge of the skewer into the bottom edge of each cake flag, then finish stitching up (see photo 5).

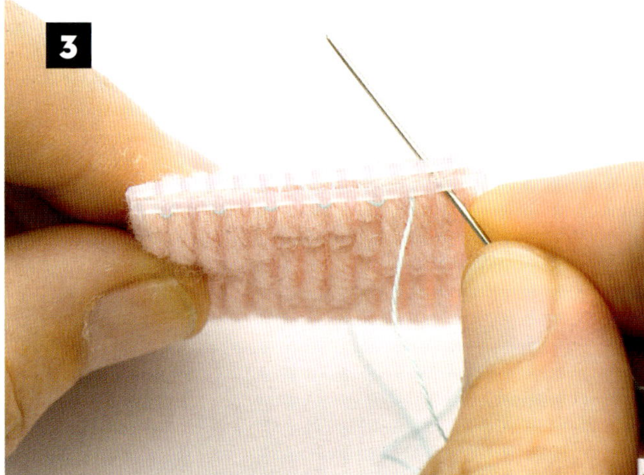

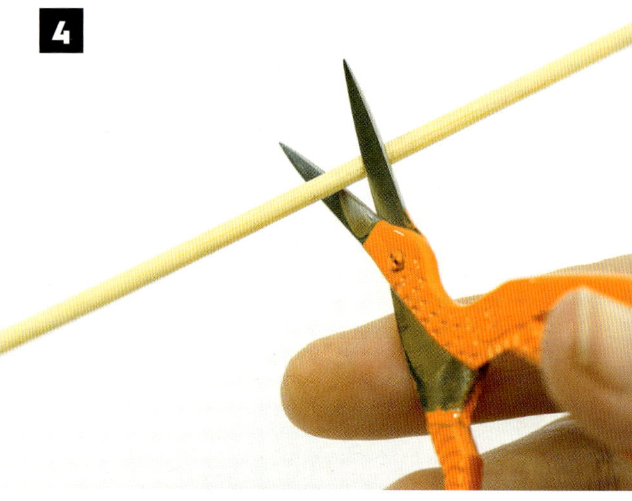

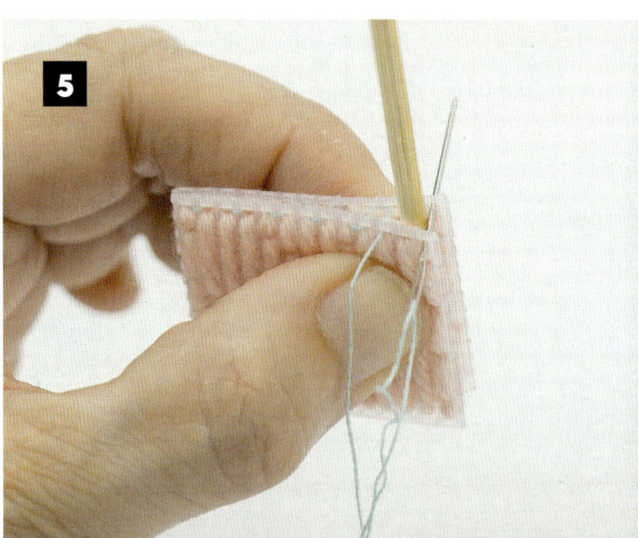

SNAZZY SNEEZERS TISSUE BOX

This vibrant cover is an eye-catching way to dress up that most humble of everyday items, the tissue box, elevating it to a work of art! I've chosen just one stitch, but it's a good one. Prepare to master the always fabulous, almost hallucinatory, movement stitch. You'll discover just how easy it is to use one stitch to build a pattern with a clever selection of colour choices.

YOU WILL NEED

- Two 27 x 34cm (10⅝ x 13⅜in) sheets of 10-ct plastic canvas
- Anchor Tapestry Wool: five skeins of colour 8002 (white); three skeins each of colours 8394 (light pink), 8454 (bright pink), 8962 (mint) and 9112 (bright green)
- Size 20 tapestry needle
- Embroidery scissors
- One square box of tissues

STITCHES USED

Movement Movement stitch.

01 First, cut your plastic canvas pieces. I've designed this cover to fit a square tissue box with sides measuring a standard size of approx 13 x 13cm (5 x 5in), but if your tissue box is larger, the chart pattern is easy enough to extend. Cut five pieces of plastic canvas (photo 1).

LIE YOUR TISSUE BOX ON A SHEET OF BLANK PAPER AND LIGHTLY TRACE AROUND IT. CUT ALONG THE TRACE LINES TO GIVE YOU A TEMPLATE TO CUT THE PLASTIC CANVAS BY, WITHOUT HAVING TO MARK THE CANVAS.

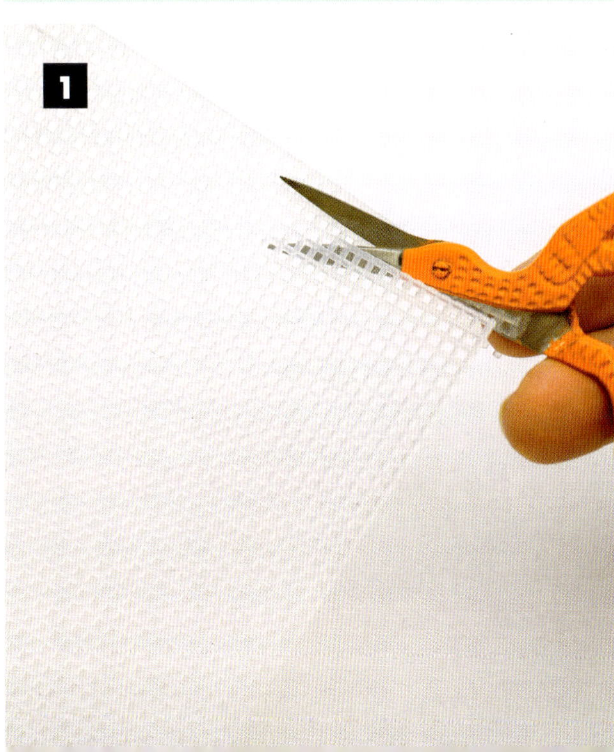

02 Take one of your cut plastic canvas pieces and prepare it to form the top of the cover. Using the chart as your guide, count and mark out the hole for the tissues. Carefully snip the bars of canvas to create the hole (see photo 2).

03 Following the chart as a guide, stitch the sides and the top with movement stitch using alternating colours to create your pattern. Photo 3 shows the first row being stitched.

MOVEMENT STITCH USES LONG STRETCHING STITCHES, SO CUT THREADS TO DOUBLE YOUR USUAL LENGTH TO SAVE FROM CASTING ON AND OFF TOO OFTEN.

04 Once the stitching of the sides and top is complete, neaten the bottom edge of each side panel and edges of the hole on the top panel with whip stitch.

05 With all your panels ready, join each of your sides panels in turn to your top panel, using whip stitch (see photo 4), and then whip stitch the sides together to complete your structure.

06 Place the cover over your tissue box and tease your tissues through the hole in the top (see photo 5).

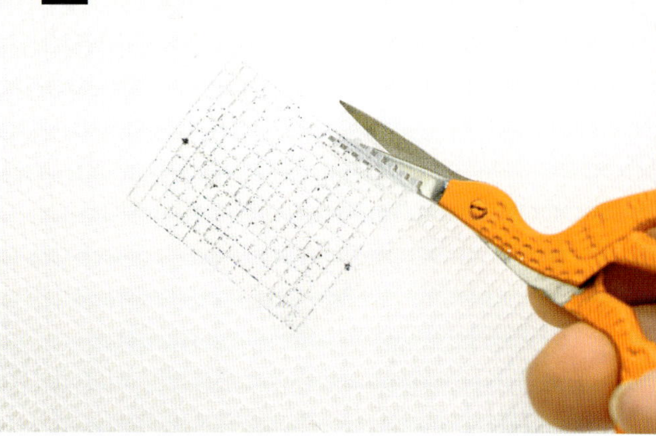

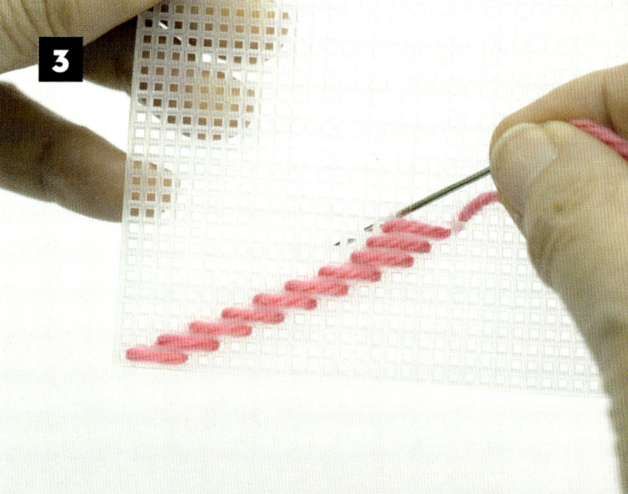

8002 8962 9112 8394 8454

TOP

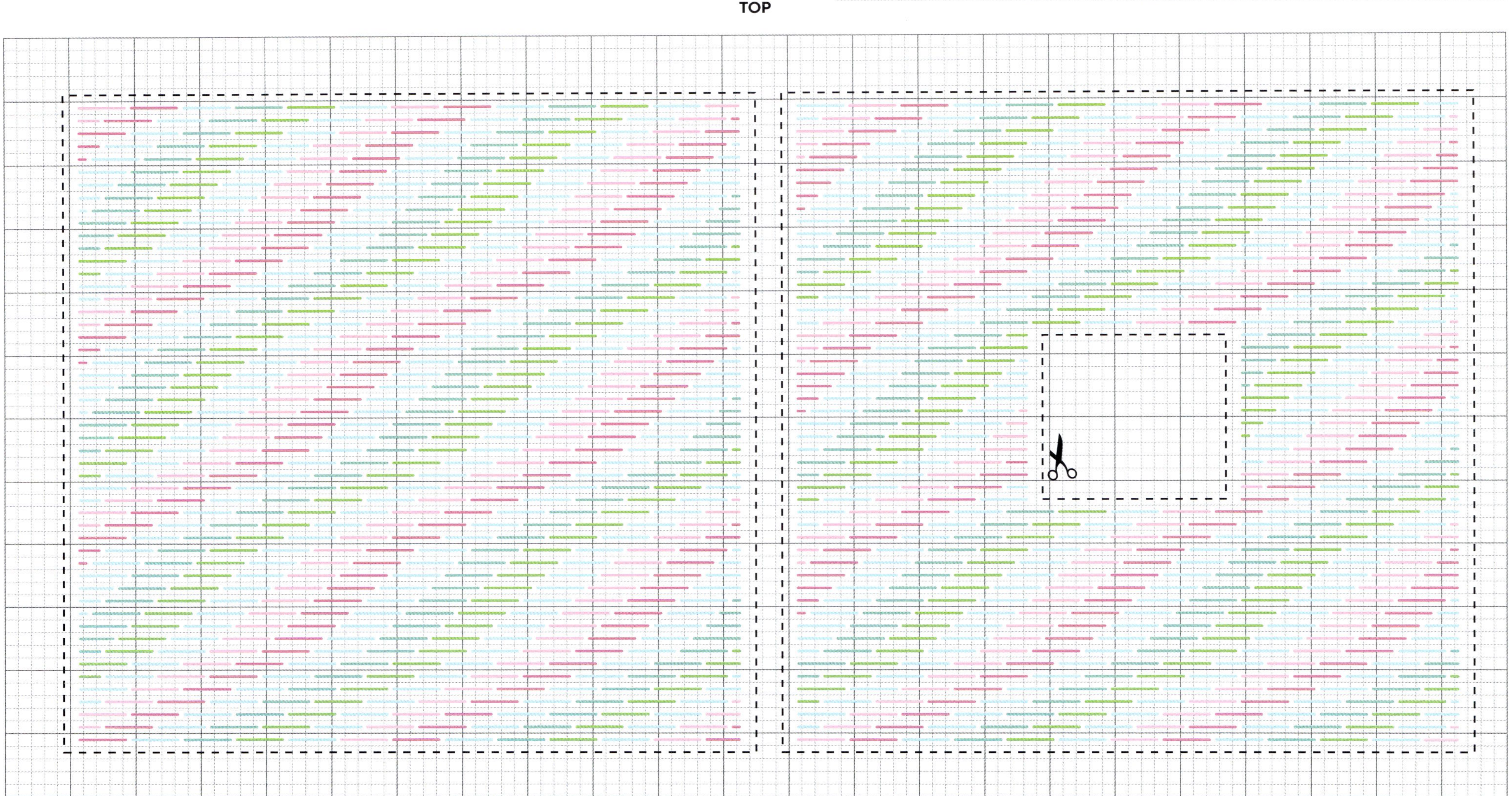

FOR THE LOVE OF FLOWERS NOTEBOOK

Bring in the botanicals with this pretty notebook cover. Be amazed at how a few long upright cross stitches can be turned into sprigs of lavender so realistic you'll almost think you can smell them! Marvel at how small brocade stitch creates a field of sunny daises. And what's not to love about the darning hearts background?

YOU WILL NEED

- Two 27 x 34cm (10⅝ x 13⅜in) sheets of 10-ct plastic canvas
- Anchor Tapestry Wool: sixteen skeins of colour 8962 (mint); one skein each of colours 8400 (maroon), 8594 (dark purple), 8590 (mid purple), 8006 (white), 8022 (yellow), 8974 (dark green), 8682 (blue) and 8872 (very light blue)
- Size 20 tapestry needle
- Embroidery scissors
- One A5 spiral-bound notebook (no more than 100 pages)

STITCHES USED

Basics Tent stitch.

Texture Small brocade stitch; Long upright cross stitch.

Borders Darning hearts.

01 Let's start by stitching the front panel of the notebook. Turning your first plastic canvas sheet to a landscape position and counting up from the bottom left-hand corner, stitch your first maroon circle in tent stitch. This will give you a great anchor point to easily count and stitch the rest of your circles (photo 1).

02 Now to fill in your circles, starting with the fields of daisies. The top left-hand circle is stitched with small brocade stitch using white tapestry wool as the dominant colour; the bottom right-hand circle is also stitched with small brocade stitch, but this time using yellow tapestry wool as the dominant colour. Following the chart, stitch the tent stitch detailing at the centre of the stitches to complete the daisies.

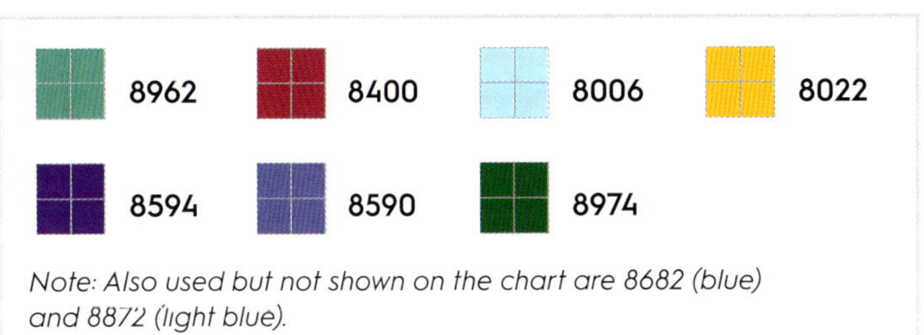
8962
8400
8006
8022
8594
8590
8974
Note: Also used but not shown on the chart are 8682 (blue) and 8872 (light blue).

03 Moving on to the lavender-filled circles and carefully following the chart, start by stitching the flower heads with long upright cross stitch, then the stems with a dark green tent stitch, and continue to fill in the rest of the circles with tent stitches in the background colour, using 8682 (blue) for the bottom left-hand circle and 8872 (very light blue) for the top right-hand circle.

04 Once the stitching of the flower circles is complete, it's time to trim the plastic canvas to the finished size of your front panel. I've included a cut line on the chart to be sure you leave enough space for the stitching of the background.

05 Take the cut-to-size partially-stitched front panel and cut a back panel from your second sheet of plastic canvas to match. Then cut two more pieces, each the same height as the front panel but only 13cm (5in) wide (these will become the inside flaps of your notebook cover).

06 Now return to the front panel to fill in the background, using darning hearts worked with mint tapestry wool. Refer to the chart for the starting position of the first heart in your first row of hearts, to ensure you line them all up evenly across the piece (see photo 2).

07 Stitch darning hearts across the whole of the back panel and the two inside flap panels, using the same starting position as before.

08 Working on a piece of the remaining plastic canvas, stitch a single column of darning hearts as shown on photo 3, then trim the edges down. This will become the spine of your notebook cover.

09 Now to join all the pieces together in a whip stitch marathon! Take the front panel and one of the inside flap panels and join them along the top, side and bottom edges to create a pocket (see photo 4). Then mirror this by joining the back panel and the remaining inside flap panel to make a second pocket.

10 Here's the trickiest bit: take the trimmed spine panel and join the front panel to its right-hand edge using whip stitch. Then join the back panel to its left-hand side. The notebook cover is now complete and you can slide your spiral-bound notebook into the inside flap pockets (photo 5).

2

3

4

5

RISE AND SHINE MIRROR FRAME

Start every day with a ray of sunshine! Made with just two simple panels this project is surprisingly easy to finish into a standing mirror ready to smarten up any dressing table. The stitch selection here explores movement in the sunrays, texture in the sun and scenic stitches as you build your clouds.

YOU WILL NEED

- Two 27 x 34cm (10⅝ x 13⅜in) sheets of 10-ct plastic canvas
- Anchor Tapestry Wool: seven skeins of 8782 (sky blue)*; two skeins each of colours 8112 (yellow) and 8134 (egg yolk yellow); one skein each of colours 8002 (white for right cloud) and 8006 (white for left cloud)
- Size 20 tapestry needle
- Embroidery scissors
- A4 size L-stand sign holder
- Self-adhesive mirror tile 15 x 15cm (6 x 6in)

*I CHOSE A VARIEGATED HAND-DYED TAPESTRY WOOL FROM THE YARN WHISPERER IN THE COLOUR 'TROPO-SPHERE'. EACH HANK IS 55M (60YD) LONG SO I NEEDED ONLY TWO SKEINS.

STITCHES USED

Basics Tent stitch.

Movement Condensed cashmere stitch variation; Double woven stitch.

Texture Kennan stitch.

Sky Swirl stitch; Double Hungarian stitch.

01 First prepare the sign holder by sticking the self-adhesive mirror tile in place, measuring down 4cm (1½in) from the top edge and making sure the tile is centralized (see photo 1).

MOST ADHESIVE TILES WILL COME WITH A STICKY BACK OR STICKY PADS TO ATTACH THEM.

1

02 Now prepare one sheet of plastic canvas for stitching. Following the chart as your guide, count and mark out the aperture for the mirror tile to show through, then carefully snip the bars of the canvas to create the hole (see photo 2).

03 Referring to the chart, stitch the egg yolk yellow sunbeam spaces with double woven stitch. I've shown you the full stitch workings on the chart. Notice how it tilts in different directions on the side spaces, and how it is mirrored on the top sunbeam (see photo 3).

04 Referring to the chart, stitch the yellow sunbeam spaces with condensed cashmere stitch variation (see photo 4). I've shown you the full stitch workings on the chart. Notice how it tilts in different directions on the side spaces.

05 Referring to the chart, stitch the left-hand cloud in double Hungarian stitch (see photo 5).

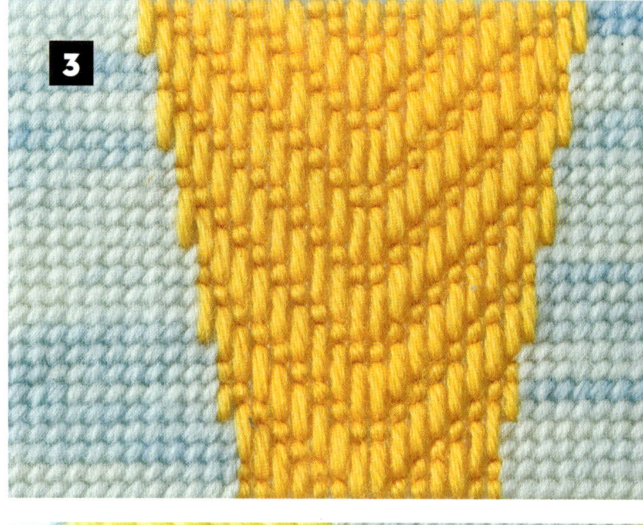

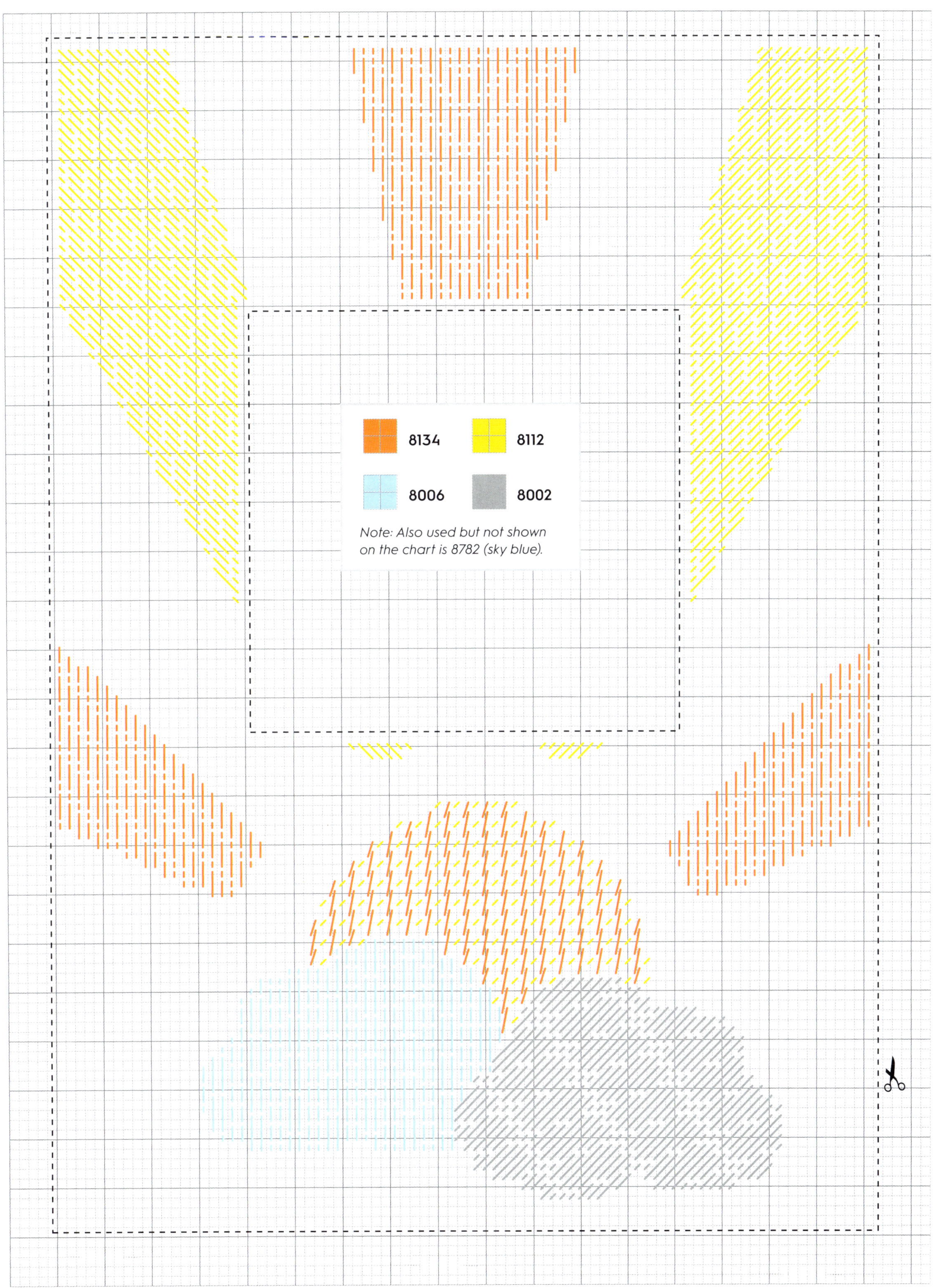
8134
8112
8006
8002
Note: Also used but not shown on the chart is 8782 (sky blue).

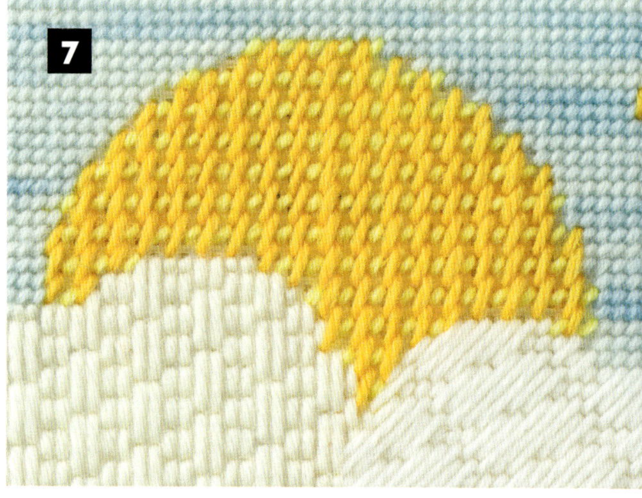

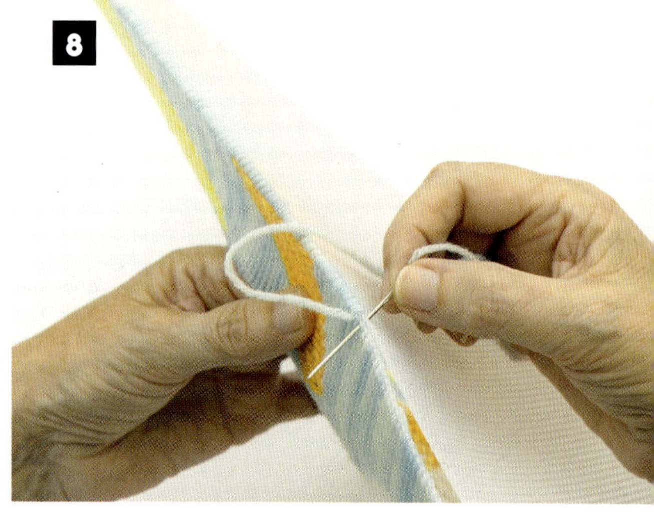

06 Referring to the chart, stitch the right-hand cloud in swirl stitch (see photo 6).

07 Finally, it's time to stitch the sun in beautiful Kennan stitch! To make it easy I've given you the full stitch workings on the chart. Just make sure to work the longer stitches in egg yolk yellow and the shorter stitches in yellow (see photo 7).

08 Starting from the bottom left-hand corner, fill in the remaining blank sections of the canvas using tent stitch and the sky blue wool.

09 Once the stitching of the front panel is complete, neaten the mirror hole and the bottom edge with whip stitch, then trim the plastic canvas at the side and top edges of the design, making sure to leave one bar of canvas clear. Before moving on to the next step, cut your back panel from the plastic canvas making sure it is three bars wider than your front panel.

10 Now we're going to join the stitched front panel to the back panel to make a sleeve. (I've left the back panel of my mirror unstitched but you could stitch it with tent stitch if you choose to; see tip for more details.) Start by joining the front and back at one of the sides (photo 8), then along the top edge, using whip stitch. Then slide the partially-joined cover over your prepared stand and carefully whip stitch the remaining side to secure it (photo 9). (If the fit isn't looking too tight, you can whip stitch in hand and slide the sleeve over your stand after you have joined your remaining side.)

IF YOU WANT TO STITCH YOUR BACK PANEL WITH TENT STITCH, YOU'LL NEED ABOUT NINE SKEINS OF ANCHOR TAPESTRY WOOL TO COVER IT.

ELEMENTAL COASTERS

Earth, air, fire and water. Which will you choose? Taking inspiration from the elements, these little mats are quick-to-stitch and make a great gift, so why not stitch them all! Each showcases a different stitch, and you'll find the repetition has you learning the stitches by heart in no time at all. They'll certainly cheer up Monday morning coffee break, especially when worked in gorgeous variegated shades.

YOU WILL NEED

- One 27 x 34cm (10⅝ x 13⅜in) sheet of 10-ct plastic canvas
- Anchor Tapestry Wool: one skein each of colours 8802 (pale blue), 8804 (light blue), 8002 (white), 8034 (cream), 8166 (orange), 8168 (dark orange), 9116 (light green) and 9118 (mid green) or variegated shades of these colours*
- Size 20 tapestry needle
- Embroidery scissors
- Felt for backing
- Fabric glue

*I CHOSE VARIEGATED HAND-DYED TAPESTRY WOOLS FROM THE YARN WHISPERER IN THE COLOURS CARIBBEAN, CUMULONIMBUS, FLAME AND FOLIAGE.

STITCHES USED

Sky Double Hungarian stitch.

Water Open wave stitch; Mini wave stitch.

Land Grass stitch.

01 Cut your canvas into four even squares approx 10.5cm (4⅛in) each.

02 Following the chart as your starting point, stitch the fire coaster in open wave stitch (see photo 1). Trim any excess canvas and whip stitch the edges once the stitching is complete.

1

03 Following the chart as your starting point, stitch the water coaster in mini wave stitch (see photo 2). Trim any excess canvas and whip stitch the edges once the stitching is complete.

04 Following the chart as your starting point, stitch the air coaster in double Hungarian stitch (see photo 3). Trim any excess canvas and whip stitch the edges once the stitching is complete.

05 Following the chart as your starting point, stitch the earth coaster in grass stitch (see photo 4). Trim any excess canvas and whip stitch the edges once the stitching is complete.

06 Cut four squares measuring 10 x 10cm (4 x 4in) from your felt, and glue one to the underside of each of the coasters with fabric glue (see photo 5).

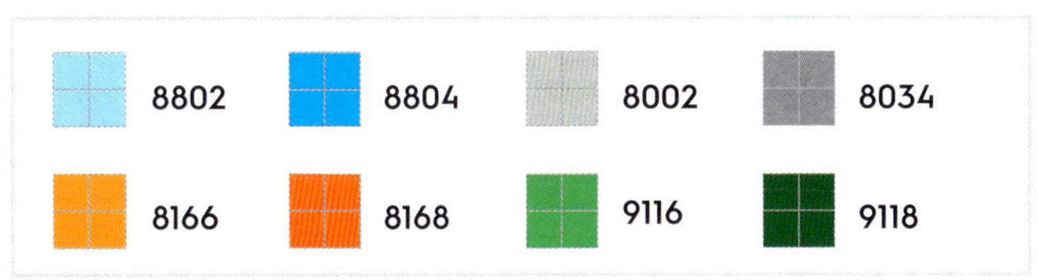
8802
8804
8002
8034
8166
8168
9116
9118

BESIDE THE SEA BEACH BAG

This glamorous purse gives the 'beach bag' a completely new vibe! It has a front window to slot your stitching into, so now you can take a part of the ocean with you wherever you go! I've used Bargello wave stitch worked in three colours to capture the tones of the sea, as the wave breaks against the shoreline stitched with sandhills stitch. This seaside scene illustrates how a couple of clever stitch choices can add movement and dimension to your stitching.

YOU WILL NEED

- One 27 x 34cm (10⅝ x 13⅜in) sheet of 10-ct plastic canvas
- Anchor Tapestry Wool: one skein each of colours 8362 (light pink), 8366 (dark pink), 8156 (orange), 8872 (very light blue), 8912 (pale blue), 9450 (dark brown), 8936 (dark aqua), 8804 (light blue), 8000 (white for sea) and 8002 (white for letter)
- Size 20 tapestry needle
- Embroidery scissors
- Acrylic bag with front window of approx 11 x 18cm (4¼ x 7in)
- Felt for backing
- Fabric glue

STITCHES USED

Basics Tent stitch.

Water Bargello wave stitch.

Land Sandhills stitch.

01 Cut a piece of plastic canvas to measure the same size as, or ever so slightly smaller than, the inside of your bag's front window (see photo 1).

TAKE A PIECE OF PAPER AND CAREFULLY TRACE AROUND THE BAG'S OUTER WINDOW IN PENCIL. THEN CUT ALONG YOUR TRACE LINES AND SEE HOW IT FITS IN THE INNER SECTION OF THE WINDOW. ADJUST THE SIZE IF NECESSARY THEN USE AS A TEMPLATE TO CUT YOUR CANVAS.

1

TOP

8000

8804

8936

8156

8362

8366

8912

8872

8002

9450

Note: Also used but not shown on the chart is 8132 (yellow)

02 The best place to start this design is by working the starfish, shells and message in a bottle, as these are all worked in simple tent stitch (see photo 2).

03 Then move on to stitch the sea. This is worked in Bargello wave stitch, with order of the yarn colours shown on the chart (see photo 3). It really helps to start with the white edge sections of the wave.

04 Once the sea is completed, fill in the beach background. I chose to stitch this in sandhills stitch, which gives a gentle movement to this area of the design in contrast to the encroaching wave. To keep the chart as clear and easy to follow as possible, this is not shown on the chart; the easiest place to start the background stitching is at the top right-hand corner to give yourself a clear run to establish the shape.

IF YOUR BAG IS SMALLER OR LARGER THAN THE ONE SHOWN, THE BACKGROUND STITCHING CAN EASILY BE EXTENDED OR CROPPED TO FIT SIZE.

05 Whip stitch the edges of the stitched canvas, then cut a piece of felt to the same size and glue it to the back (see photo 4). Slip the canvas into the window at the front of the bag as seen in photo 5, and you're ready to go!

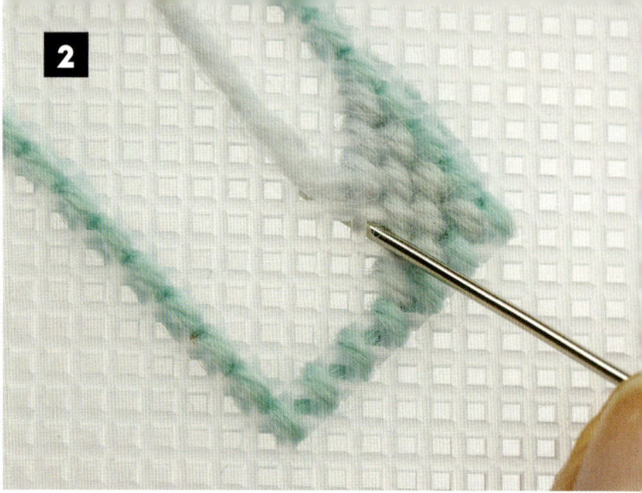
2

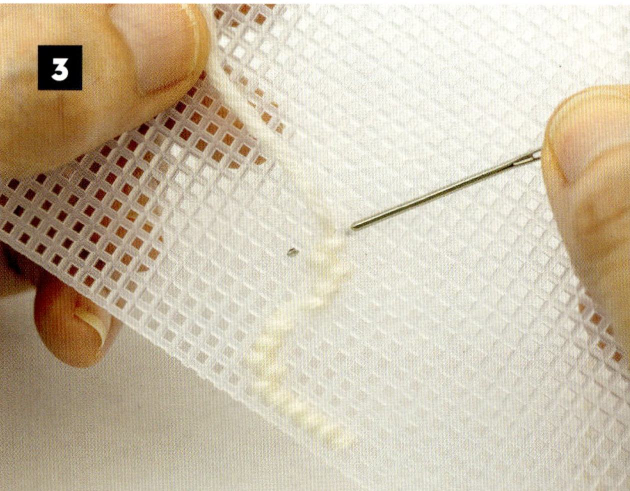
3

4

5

PERFECT PICNIC NAPKIN RINGS

Add a touch of whimsy to your picnics and dinner parties with these needlepoint napkin rings! Perfect for year round use, they'll bring back memories of summertime picnics in the park. See how triple Hungarian stitch makes a cute cloud pattern, to pair brilliantly with a flower meadow created by using double V with upright crosses.

YOU WILL NEED

- One 27 x 34cm (10⅝ x 13⅜in) sheet of 10-ct plastic canvas
- Anchor Tapestry Wool: one skein each of colours 8774 (blue), 8002 (white), 9164 (green), 8132 (yellow) and 8156 (orange)
- Size 20 tapestry needle
- Embroidery scissors
- Felt for backing
- Fabric glue

STITCHES USED

Sky Triple Hungarian stitch.

Land Double V with upright crosses.

01 Starting at the bottom left-hand corner of your canvas, cast on ready to begin the cloud napkin ring design. This is worked in triple Hungarian stitch and the stitch placement is fully shown on the chart (see photo 1). You may prefer to park your threads rather than cast off each time a colour change is required.

THE TAPESTRY WOOL REQUIREMENTS GIVEN ARE SUFFICIENT TO MAKE ONE OF EACH NAPKIN RING DESIGN.

1

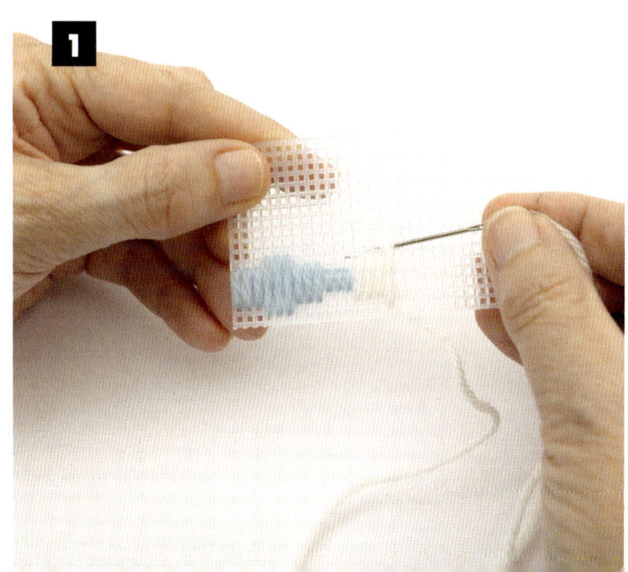

YOU COULD CUT YOUR CANVAS SHAPES OUT FIRST, AS I HAVE DONE IN THE PHOTOS, AND JUST FILL THEM IN WITH YOUR STITCHES.

02 Once you have completed stitching the cloud napkin ring design, leave a space of eight canvas holes and begin stitching the flower meadow napkin ring design directly below. This is worked in double V with upright crosses and the stitch placement is fully shown on the chart (see photo 2). I find it easier to stitch all of the green leaves first, then the flowers.

03 Once the stitching of the napkin rings is complete, it's time to trim your plastic canvas, leaving four holes of canvas at one end, as shown on the chart, and one bar of canvas all the way around the remaining three edges (see photo 3).

04 Whip stitch around three edges of the trimmed pieces, but leave the end with the extra rows of holes for now.

05 Now cut two pieces of felt to line your napkin rings with. Place the stitched canvas on top of your felt and cut around it, trimming it slightly so that it is about one canvas hole shorter than the whip-stitched edges and about 2.5cm (1in) shorter than the end with the extra rows of holes (photo 4). Don't glue the felt in place yet, as you've one more bit of stitching to do first.

06 Take each of your stitched napkin rings in turn and roll to join the short ends together by whip stitching along the edges of the design, making sure that the four empty canvas rows at the one end are tucked inside the ring shape (see photo 5). This creates a lip that gives your napkin rings structure and keeps them in a perfect circle. Cast off by running the thread carefully through the back of your stitches.

07 Gently dab dots of fabric glue on one side of the felt lining pieces, then carefully place them inside the rings, smoothing them down.

2

3

4

5

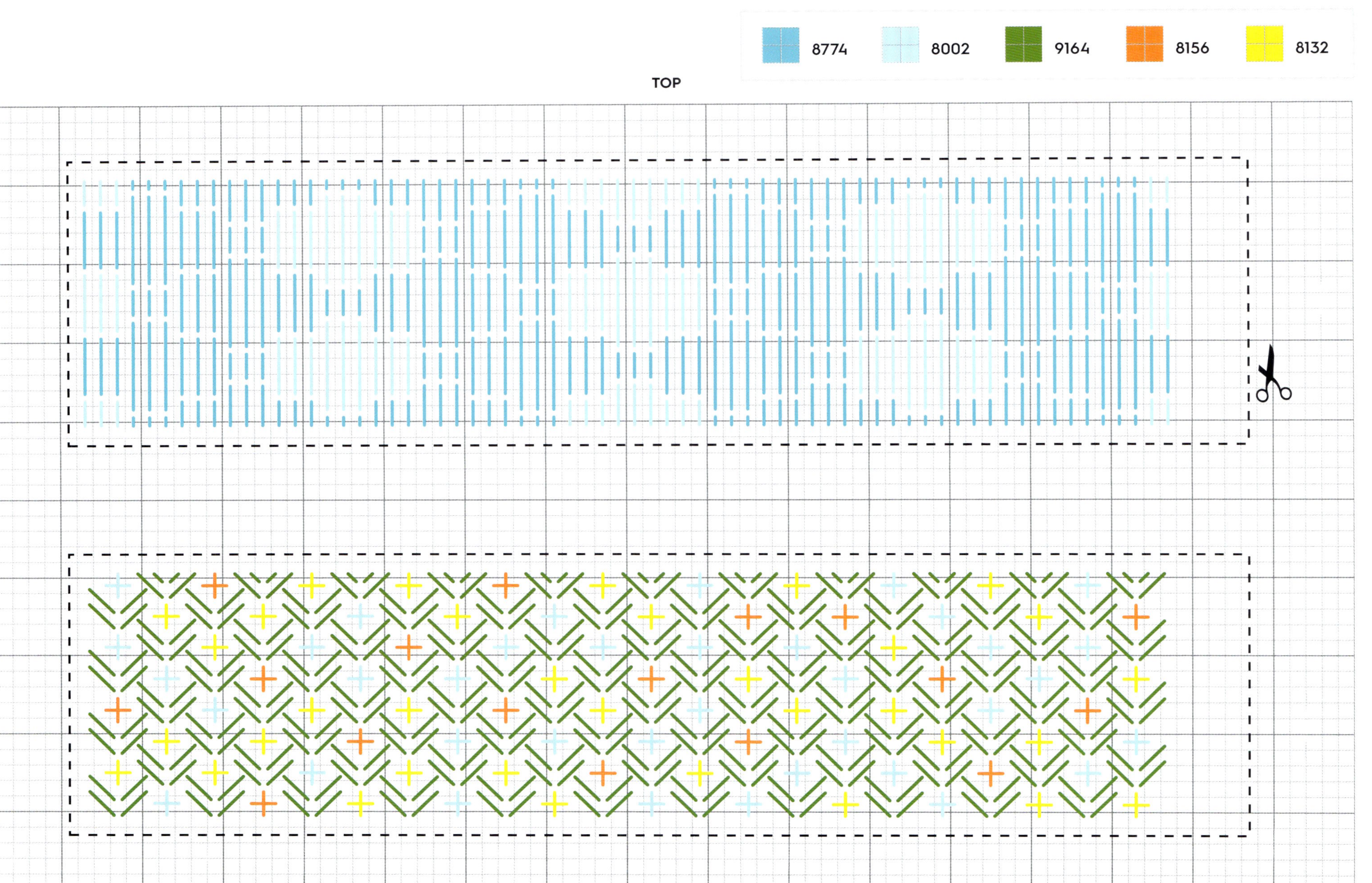
8774
8002
9164
8156
8132
TOP

LITTLE TREASURES TRINKET TRAY

Always have a safe spot to keep your prized possessions in with this delightful trinket tray. You'll see how a border stitch like Roman cross can stand perfectly on its own to create the outer walls of your container. Paired with purple balloon stitch for the base, this design has a distinctly fruity feel!

YOU WILL NEED

- One 27 x 34cm (10⅝ x 13⅜in) sheet of 10-ct plastic canvas
- Anchor Tapestry Wool: one skein each of colours 8594 (dark purple), 8590 (mid purple), 8974 (dark green) and 9164 (light green)
- DMC stranded cotton (floss): one skein of colour 907 (lime green)
- Size 20 tapestry needle
- Size 6 or 8 embroidery needle
- Embroidery scissors
- Felt for lining the base
- Fabric glue

STITCHES USED

Texture Balloon stitch.

Borders Roman cross.

01 Start by stitching your side panels. You are going to stitch four of the short side panels and four of the long side panels (photo 1) using Roman cross, following the stitch placement shown on the chart.

I FIND LEAVING THREE OR MORE ROWS OF EMPTY CANVAS AROUND EACH STITCHED PIECE MAKES IT EASY TO TRIM LATER.

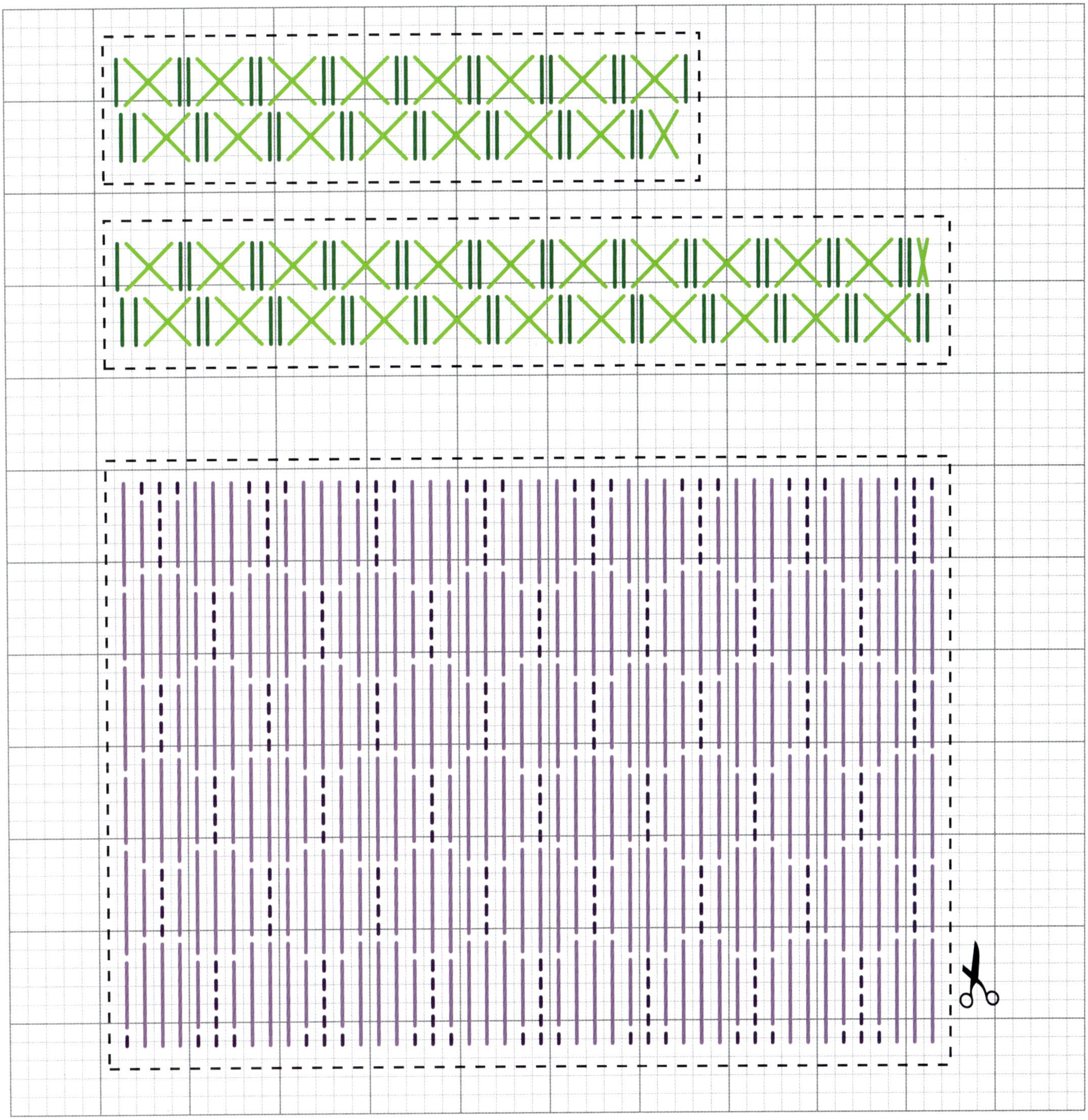

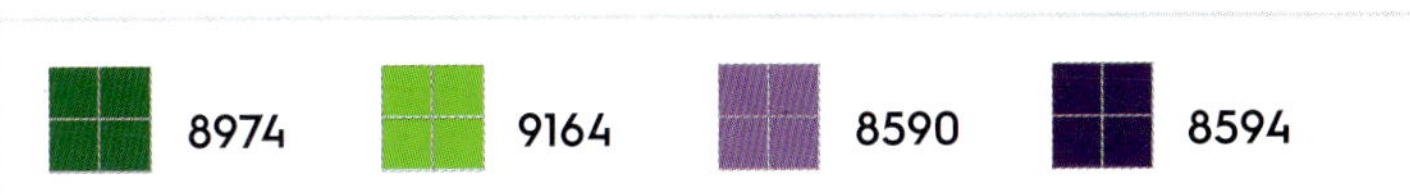
8974
9164
8590
8594

02 Now to stitch the base. Start by stitching the balloon stitches in mid purple, as shown on the chart (photo 2). Then in between each balloon stitch, work four little straight stitches in dark purple, each crossing one bar of canvas, as shown on the chart.

03 Once the stitching is complete, it's time to trim your plastic canvas, leaving one bar of canvas all the way around the edge (see photo 3).

04 Now to sew your pieces together to make the trinket tray, starting by making the side panels, which are doubled up to give your trinket tray a good firm structure to safely contain all your treasures! Thread the embroidery needle with a length of stranded cotton (floss), just one strand is perfect, and pairing up the short side panels with wrong sides together, join each pair using a running stitch zigging in and out of the very edge of the canvas holes (photo 4). Join the long side panels in the same way.

05 Now join each of your side panels to the base, again using whip stitch and stranded cotton (floss). Once each side panel is in place, you can join the side panels together to make the corners of your trinket tray.

06 Cut a piece of felt to the same size as the base of the trinket tray. Lightly dab fabric glue onto the felt, line up the base of the trinket box and press in place (photo 5).

CUTE CARD KEEPER WALLET

By using Albemarle stitch to build up an eye-catching stripy pattern alongside a bold shadow mesh band, this practical little wallet becomes a feast for the eyes. Your bank cards will now have such a stylish home that you'll be looking for excuses to get them out of your pocket!

YOU WILL NEED

- One 27 x 34cm (10⅝ x 13⅜in) sheet of 10-ct plastic canvas
- Anchor Tapestry Wool: one skein each of colours 8112 (yellow), 8962 (mint), 8154 (orange), 8400 (maroon) and 8304 (peach)
- Size 20 tapestry needle
- Embroidery scissors
- One flex frame approx 10cm (4in) long

STITCHES USED

Basics Tent stitch.

Movement Albemarle stitch.

Borders Shadow mesh.

01 We're going to start in the bottom left-hand corner and use Albemarle stitch, as shown in the chart. Alternate the colours for each diagonal stripe using yellow, peach and orange (see photo 1). You'll notice that I have flipped the direction of the stitch at the middle so that it mirrors.

02 Now for a band of shadow mesh in mint and maroon, as shown on the chart.

THIS PROJECT IS ONE WHERE YOU'LL WANT TO PARK YOUR THREADS, TO SAVE YOU CASTING OFF EACH TIME A COLOUR CHANGE IS REQUIRED.

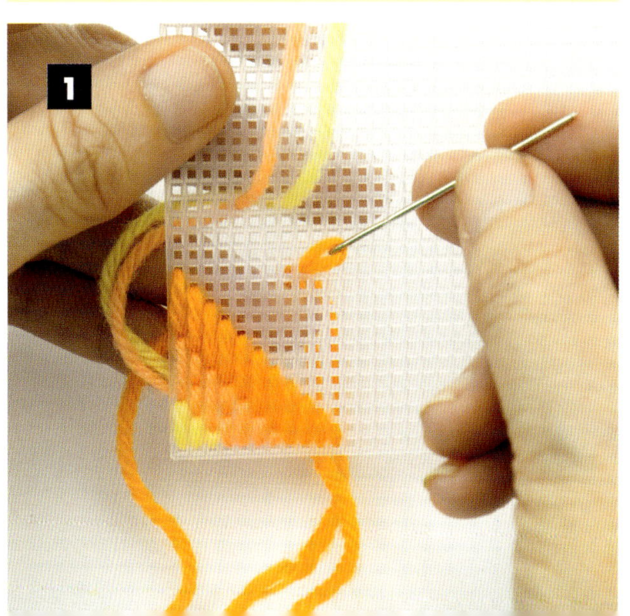

03 Finish stitching the front panel of your card keeper with an orange zigzag that echoes the Albemarle stitch, and border it with a line of tent stitches in peach. Fill in the gaps between your tent stitch border and your orange zigzag with small peach straight stitches.

04 Stitch a second (back) panel in the same way starting at least five canvas holes distance away from your first. Once the stitching is complete, trim both panels leaving one bar of canvas around three sides and leaving six empty rows of holes at the top edge, as shown in the chart.

05 Carefully slide the pin out of one end of your flex frame and put it safely to the side making sure not to lose it (photo 2).

FLEX FRAMES WORK BY APPLYING PRESSURE AT BOTH ENDS TO POP THEM OPEN, AND WHEN YOU RELEASE THEM THEY CLOSE.

06 Take one of your stitched panels and using a length of yellow tapestry wool, bring your needle up through the canvas hole shared with the top of the peach row of tent stitches, taking your wool up over five bars of canvas in a straight line. As you bring your wool back up through your next tent stitch, make sure to trap the flex frame at the back (photo 3).

07 Repeat step 6 to join the second stitched panel to the other arm of the flex frame while it is still un-hinged on one end.

08 Now gently replace the pin in the open end of your flex frame and bend the metal shut - you should be able to do this with your fingers, but you can always use mini pliers or even a pair of tweezers to do the job (photo 4). I've shown this in isolation so you can easily see where the pin goes.

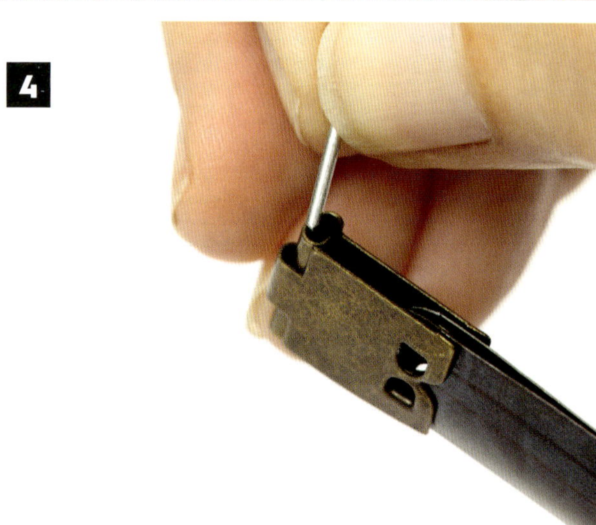

09 Whip stitch your edges together with peach wool and also whip stitch along the top edge of each panel, above the yellow stitches that are holding the flex frame arms in place, for the neatest finish (photo 5).

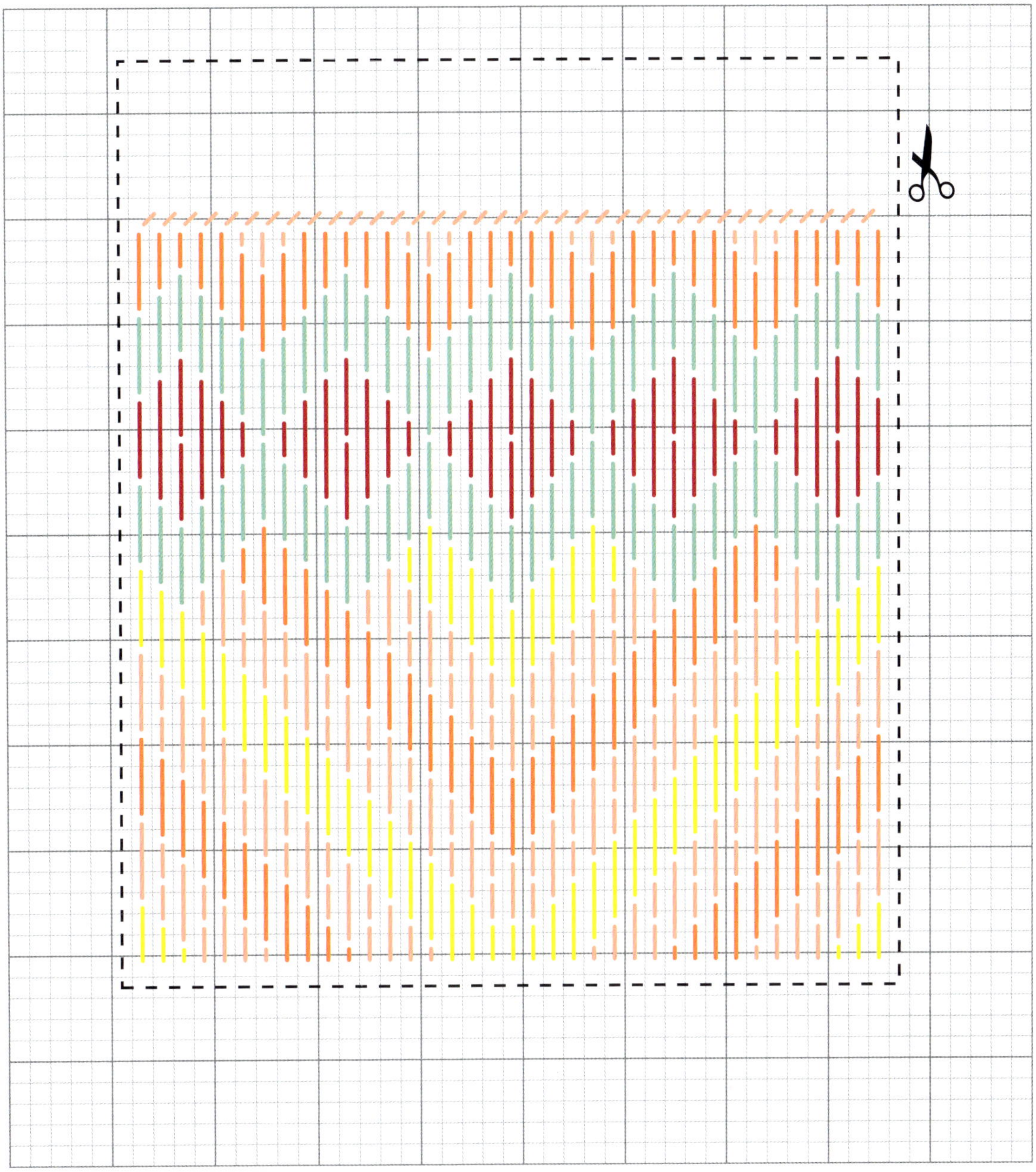

8304
8154
8962
8400
8112

THREAD CONVERSION CHART

All the projects in this book are stitched using my preferred Anchor Tapestry Wool, but if you find DMC more readily available in your area, simply use this handy conversion chart to find the comparable shades.

Anchor	DMC
8000	Snow
8002	White
8006	Ecru
8022	7474
8092	7049
8112	7049
8118	7973
8132	0701
8134	7917

Anchor	DMC
8156	7740
8166	7053
8254	7762
8362	7132
8366	7202
8392	7003
8394	7004
8400	7196
8432	7004
8454	7603

Anchor	DMC
8586	7241
8590	7025
8594	7022
8682	7800
8782	7031
8802	7828
8804	7036
8872	7928
8912	7599
8936	7926

Anchor	DMC
8962	7958
8974	7914
8988	7911
9096	7382
9112	7041
9116	7042
9118	7344
9450	7700
9488	7463
9800	Black

ABOUT THE AUTHOR

Emma Homent is the creative brain behind modern craft brand, The Makers Marks. Known for her love of colour, Emma's designs fuse the cute retro regalia she's nostalgic for with a contemporary aesthetic.

She has had an almost lifelong love affair with needlepoint, having been taught it at the age of six years old by her mum, who was desperate to find something to get the bouncy young Emma to sit still for a bit, and it was a great success!

In 2020 Emma launched the popular #stitchmondays, a weekly Instagram showcase of the huge variety of needlepoint stitches out there.

Her first book, *Needlepoint: A Modern Stitch Directory*, was published in 2022, closely followed by its hugely popular stitch cards edition.

Emma is a regular contributor to craft magazines.

www.themakersmarks.co.uk
www.instagram.com/themakersmarks

SUPPLIERS

To find most of the needlepoint accessories featured in this book, head to my website.

To find the wooden thread organizer, go to **www.etsy.com/uk/shop/ThreadandMercury**

UK

www.themakersmarks.co.uk

www.lakesideneedlecraft.co.uk

www.lovecrafts.com

www.yarnwhisperer.co.uk

www.folkestoneharbouryarn.com

USA

www.kcneedlepoint.com

www.shopneedlepointjunction.com

AUSTRALIA

www.allthreads.com.au

ACKNOWLEDGEMENTS

THANK YOU. . .

To Martin & Cinnamon, MIL & FIL, and Jess, for being excellent sounding boards. Especially Cinnamon, whose insights were invaluable.

To my ride or die Amanda, stitch life is so much more fun when you're around.

Thanks to my Work From Home Folk for listening to my constant mumbles about stitches and my Misfits & Muddlers for cheering me on.

To Jenny H, your popcorn creativity really helped unlock my plan for this book.

And to Ame, Lucy, Cheryl, Sam and the whole team at David and Charles, thanks for joining me in another adventure in stitches.

INDEX

A DAVID AND CHARLES BOOK

David and Charles is an imprint of David and Charles, Ltd
Suite A, Tourism House, Pynes Hill, Exeter, EX2 5WS

EU GPSR Authorised Representative:
Logos Europe, 9 rue Nicolas Poussin, 17000, La Rochelle, France
Email: contact@logoseurope.eu

First published in the UK and USA in 2025

A catalogue record for this book is available from the British Library.

ISBN-13: 9781446314029 paperback
ISBN-13: 9781446314043 EPUB

This book has been printed on paper from approved suppliers and made from pulp from sustainable sources.

Printed in China through Asia Pacific Offset for:
David and Charles, Ltd
Suite A, Tourism House, Pynes Hill, Exeter, EX2 5WS

10 9 8 7 6 5 4

Publishing Director: Ame Verso
Publishing Manager: Jeni Chown
Project Editor: Cheryl Brown
Lead Designer: Sam Staddon
Designer: Lucy Ridley
Design and Illustrations: Sarah Rowntree
Photography: Jason Jenkins
Photography and Styling: Tom Hargreaves
Pre-press Designer: Susan Reansbury
Production Manager: Beverley Richardson

David and Charles publishes high-quality books on a wide range of subjects. For more information visit www.davidandcharles.com.

Share your makes with us on social media using #dandcbooks and follow us on Facebook and Instagram by searching for @dandcbooks.

Layout of the digital edition of this book may vary depending on reader hardware and display settings.